Creative TRADITIONAL QUILTMAKING

KAREN FAIL

A J.B. Fairfax Press Publication

CONTENTS

FOREWORD

Quiltmaking has captured the imagination of people all over the world. In an
unprecedented revival of this craft over the last twenty years, many are
discovering their own creativity, as they design and make quilts using
wonderfully coloured and patterned fabrics.
Initially used as a technique for making essential bed covers, quiltmaking
now has become an irresistable pastime for those captivated
by quilts both old and new.
The quilts in this book capture something of the heritage inherent in quiltmaking,
using traditional geometric blocks and worked by hand. Once you have mastered
the techniques required for hand-piecing and appliqué, you too will delight in
making these treasures, your future heirlooms.

THE QUILTS

When my daughter Abby's team was new to netball, many mothers and fathers found it extremely difficult not to become expert coaches from the sidelines, calling out encouraging – and not so encouraging – comments. To avoid this, we resorted to reading the paper, sticking our noses in a good book or, in my case, becoming engrossed in my patchwork. This was how I first met Ros Stinson, a keen quilter and craftswoman and fellow parent of a budding netballer.

Ros was as enthusiastic about quilting as I was and immediately arranged for her friends to take a class with me. This was one of the easiest lessons I had ever given, because these ladies were already talented craftspeople involved in a broad spectrum of crafts. In time, many of Ros's tennis friends became patchworkers and eventually formed the Mirrabooka Quilters.

While making excursions into other styles of quiltmaking, the Mirrabooka Quilters still enjoy making quilts the traditional way, hand-piecing and hand-quilting their quilts that will no doubt become treasured heirlooms.

Karen

SUNFLOWERS

By Jenny Searle

With my collection of blue and yellow fabrics bulging out of its allotted space in my workroom, while the green and maroon collection languished for lack of attention, I decided to use some of my favourites and make a traditional quilt for my daughter. The Sunflower pattern promised to use some of my accumulated fabrics but I just had to buy the wonderful sunflower fabric and add it to my collection.

FINISHED SIZE

Quilt: 193 cm (77 in) square
Block size: 30 cm (12 in) square
Total number of blocks: sixteen

Hand-pieced and hand-quilted

FABRIC QUANTITIES

20 cm (8 in) of at least sixteen yellow fabrics (the more yellows you include, the scrappier the look)
Small pieces of terracotta-coloured fabric for the centre of the flowers (use as many different terracottas as you have in your scrap bag)
2 m (2^1/$_4$ yd) of blue fabric for the background
1.6 m (1^3/$_4$ yd) of navy and yellow print fabric for the sashing
70 cm (28 in) of terracotta-coloured fabric for the borders
2 m (2^1/$_4$ yd) of sunflower print fabric for the wide border
2 m (2^1/$_4$ yd) of blue fabric for the outer border and binding
4 m (4^1/$_2$ yd) of fabric for the backing
200 cm (80 in) of wadding

NOTIONS

Template plastic
Fineline permanent marker pen
Sandpaper board
Pencil B
Matching sewing threads (terracotta, yellow and blue)
Pair of compasses (optional)
Fabric scissors
Paper scissors
Thin cardboard
Quilting thread
Betweens needles, size 9 or 10, for piecing and quilting
Safety pins (approximately 350)
Quilting hoop
Large square ruler, rotary cutter and board, or thick cardboard
Sewing machine

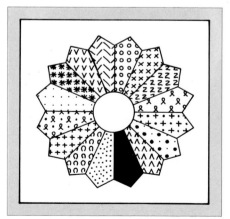

Block Diagram

MAKING TEMPLATES

See the templates on page 9. Note that the template patterns do not include seam allowances.

Trace templates A and B onto the template plastic, using the marker pen or the pencil. Mark the grain line on each template, then cut out the templates using the paper scissors. It may be easier to draw your own circle with a 3 cm (1^1/$_4$ in) radius, using the compass, than to try and accurately trace the one given. Cut sixteen B from the thin cardboard. Cut these out very carefully to give a perfect circle for the centre of each flower.

CUTTING

STEP ONE

Note that the measurements for the borders and bindings include seam allowances of 6 mm (^{1}/$_4$ in).

Cut the terracotta fabric into 4 cm (1^1/$_2$ in) wide strips across the width of the fabric.

Cut the sunflower print fabric into 15.2 cm (6 in) wide strips down the length of the fabric.

From the blue fabric for the border and binding, cut four 6.2 cm x 200 cm (2^1/$_2$ in x 80 in) strips down the length of the fabric. Cut four 9 cm x 200 cm (3^1/$_2$ in x 80 in) strips for the binding.

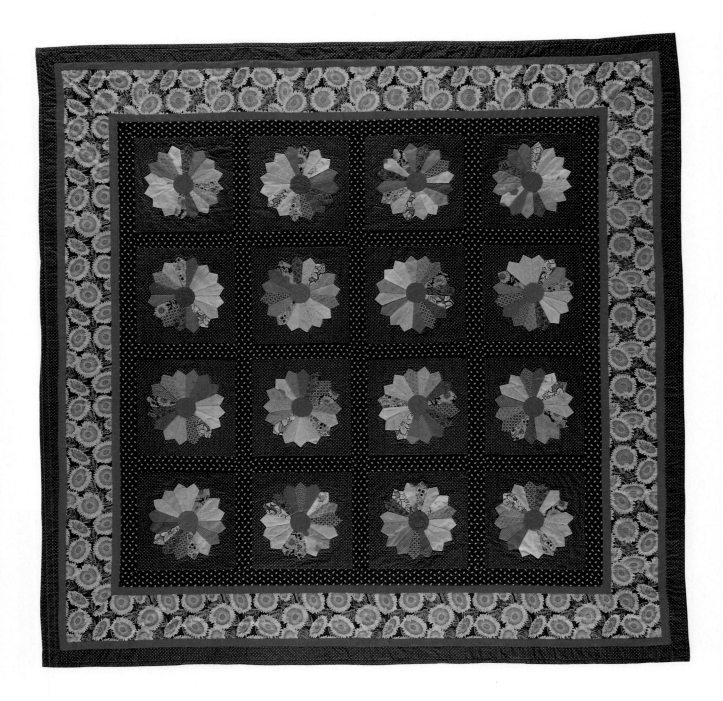

STEP TWO

Using the blue background fabric and the large square ruler, rotary cutter and board, cut out sixteen 31.2 cm (12$\frac{1}{2}$ in) squares. This measurement includes a 6 mm ($\frac{1}{4}$ in) seam allowance. If you don't have a rotary cutter and square ruler, draft a 30 cm (12 in) square on thick cardboard and use this as a template to cut out the sixteen background squares. Trace carefully around the template, leaving space between each square to allow for seams. This pencil line will be your sewing line. Cut out each square approximately 6 mm ($\frac{1}{4}$ in) from the sewing line.

STEP THREE

For each block you will need sixteen A from a variety of yellow fabrics and one terracotta B. When cutting out the terracotta circles, leave 1.5 cm ($\frac{5}{8}$ in) seam allowance outside the sewing line to enable the fabric to be basted to the cardboard.

HINT: If you are using only sixteen different yellows you will need to cut out sixteen petals from each fabric. However, you may include as many different yellows as you like, even if they only occur once in the quilt. This adds to the interest and appeal of the quilt.

STEP FOUR

For the sashing, using the navy and yellow print fabric, cut four 6.2 cm x 155 cm (2$\frac{1}{2}$ in x 62 in) pieces down the length of the fabric, three 6.2 cm x 139 cm (2$\frac{1}{2}$ in x 56 in) down the length of the fabric, and twelve 6.2 cm x 31.2 cm (2$\frac{1}{2}$ in x 12$\frac{1}{2}$ in) for the short sashing pieces.

PIECING

STEP ONE

Fold each petal over double, lengthwise, with the right sides together. Stitch across the top on the sewing line. Cut off the corner of the seam allowance nearest to the fold, then turn the petal to the right side. Push out the point neatly and press it flat. Make sixteen petals for each block.

STEP TWO

Join the sixteen petals together, arranging the colours randomly, or you could arrange the yellows from light to dark as Jenny has done.

STEP THREE

Baste a terracotta circle over a cardboard circle. Appliqué it in the centre of the pieced flower, using the terracotta thread and a small slipstitch. (For more information on appliqué see page 76.) Remove the basting and take out the cardboard through the small hole in the centre of the flower.

STEP FOUR

Find the centre of the background square by folding it in half twice and finger-pressing the folds. Centre the completed flower on the background square and secure it with pins. Appliqué the flower in place, using the yellow thread and a small slipstitch. Make sixteen blocks in the same way.

STEP FIVE

Join four blocks in a row, alternating them with small sashing strips. Join the rows, alternating them with the 139 cm (56 in) long sashing strips to form the pieced centre of the quilt.

STEP SIX

Attach the 155 cm (62 in) sashing strips around the pieced centre, mitring the corners.

FOR THE BORDERS

STEP ONE

Join the 4 cm (1$\frac{1}{2}$ in) wide strips of terracotta fabric to form four 160 cm (64 in) long pieces. Sew these to each side of the pieced top, finishing with mitred corners.

STEP TWO

Trim each sunflower fabric strip to be 191 cm (75 in) long. Sew a sunflower border to each side of the quilt top, mitring the corners.

Sewing a petal

The sunflower block

STEP THREE

Join the remaining terracotta strips to form four 193 cm (77 in) long strips. Attach one to each side of the quilt top, finishing with mitred corners.

STEP FOUR

Sew on the blue borders to complete the quilt top, mitring the corners.

ASSEMBLING

STEP ONE

Cut the backing fabric in half to give two 2 m (2¼ yd) lengths. Remove the selvages, then rejoin the pieces length-wise to give a 200 cm x 220 cm (80 in x 88 in) backing piece. Trim 10 cm (4 in) from either side of this backing piece to make it 200 cm (80 in) square.

STEP TWO

Place the backing fabric face down with the wadding on top and the quilt top on top of that, face upwards. Smooth out each layer as it is put down. Keeping the three layers as flat as possible, pin them together at about 10 cm (4 in) intervals.

QUILTING

STEP ONE

Hand- or machine-quilt around each block along the seam line (in-the-ditch). This will hold the quilt sandwich together while the hand-quilting is being completed.

STEP TWO

Hand-quilt as desired. Jenny has echo-quilted each flower and quilted a circle in each centre.

FINISHING

STEP ONE

Carefully trim the wadding and the backing to the size of the quilt top.

STEP TWO

Press the binding strips over double, lengthwise. Find the centre of the binding strip and of the quilt sides by folding. Machine-stitch the binding to the right side of the quilt, matching the centres. Mitre the corners of the binding.

STEP THREE

Turn the folded edge of the binding to the back of the quilt and slipstitch it into place. Mitre the corners on the back and finish by hand.

Don't forget to sign and date your quilt.

The three mitred borders

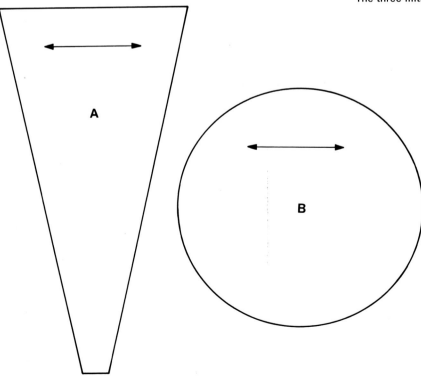

LUCKY ME

By Sue Manchip

I made twelve Inner City blocks in light, medium and dark green for a 'Block of
the Quarter' competition and was lucky enough to win one hundred blocks.
I decided to add to them to make a whole quilt. My supply of green fabrics grew,
as I made half-blocks for the sides and the chevron border. So, lucky me,
I now have a great collection of green fabrics and a new quilt!

FINISHED SIZE

Quilt: approximately 145 cm x 210 cm
(57$\frac{1}{2}$ in x 83$\frac{1}{4}$ in)
Block size: made up of three 3 cm
(1$\frac{1}{4}$ in) hexagons
Total number of complete blocks:
one hundred and twelve

Hand-pieced and hand-quilted

FABRIC QUANTITIES

Scraps of green fabric in light,
medium and dark tones
10 cm (4 in) of mid-green plain fabric
2.2 m (2$\frac{1}{2}$ yd) of dark green fabric
for the borders and binding
3.2 m (3$\frac{5}{8}$ yd) of fabric for the backing
155 cm x 220 cm (61 in x 86$\frac{1}{2}$ in)
of wadding

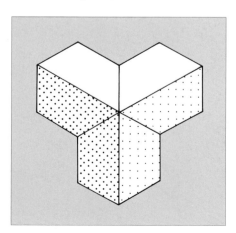

Block diagram

NOTIONS

Template plastic
Fineline permanent marker pen
Sandpaper board
Pencil, B
Pencil for marking dark fabrics, silver
or yellow
Matching sewing thread
Quilting thread, green
Fabric scissors
Glass-headed pins
Betweens needles, size 9 or 10, for
piecing and quilting
Long thin needle for basting
Quilting hoop
Safety pins
Masking tape
Firm paper or light cardboard

MAKING TEMPLATES

See the templates on page 13. Note
that the templates do not include
seam allowances.

Trace templates A, B, Br, C and D
onto the template plastic with the
marker pen. Mark the grain line on
the templates. Note that template B
provides the shape for template Br.
Trace a second template B, turn it over
and mark it Br, giving you the mirror
image of template B.

CUTTING

STEP ONE

Place the fabric on the sandpaper
board, wrong side up. With the grain
lines matching, carefully trace two of
template A from each scrap, noting
that you will need two light, two
medium and two dark half-hexagons
for each complete block.

Cut sufficient pieces for one hundred and twelve blocks. Pin together
the two light, two medium and two
dark half-hexagons that you have
chosen for each block.
HINT: You may choose to cut out each
block as you go, rather than cut them
all out at the beginning, especially if
friends happen to give you some of
their treasured greens or, of course,
you add to your own supply.

The corner detail

For the chevron border, cut the following pieces: from each of seventy-two fabrics, cut one B and one Br (use as many different greens as you can), and eight C and four D from the mid-green plain fabric.

PIECING

STEP ONE

For each block, make three hexagons, using light and dark A, light and medium A and dark and medium A to form the three hexagons. Join them together, keeping the darks on the left side, the mediums on the right side and the lights on the third side. Use the photographs and the block diagram as a guide. Make one hundred and twelve blocks.

HINT: You may wish to join the hexagons using the English piecing method. Cut six half-hexagons from firm paper or light cardboard exactly the size of the template. Cut six half-hexagons from light, medium and dark fabric, as above, including at least a 12 mm (^{1}/$_2$ in) seam allowance. Wrap the fabric around the paper or cardboard and baste them into place. With the wrong sides together and carefully

The completed chevron border

matching the corners, whipstitch two hexagons together, using a matching thread. Repeat for each hexagon keeping the light, medium and dark as indicated in the block diagram. Assemble the blocks, then join the blocks to make the quilt top in a similar manner. The paper or cardboard is removed once the entire quilt is assembled.

STEP TWO

Keeping the darks on the left side, sew the completed blocks together, forming the central section of the quilt top. This section is eight blocks wide and fourteen blocks long. To make this section rectangular, add partial blocks as required, keeping the pattern of darks on the left side. Use the photographs as a guide.

STEP THREE

To assemble the long chevron border, sew twenty-four different B shapes together to form a long strip. Sew the matching Br shapes cut from the same fabric together to form a similar long strip. Sew the strips together, lengthwise, to form the chevron, matching shapes from the same fabric. Sew two C pieces to the end of the chevron strip. Continue in a similar manner to form the other half of the chevron border, making sure that you reverse the chevron direction. Make two. Use the photograph and figure 1 as a guide. For the short chevron border, use fourteen B and Br shapes before adding the two C pieces and reversing the chevron direction. Make two. Attach a mid-green square (D) to both ends of the short chevron border strips.

STEP FOUR

Using the dark green border fabric, cut down the length of the fabric:
two 11.2 cm x 144 cm (4^1/$_2$ in x 56^3/$_4$ in) strips for the inner borders;
two 11.2 cm x 96 cm (4^1/$_2$ in x 38^1/$_2$ in) strips for the inner borders;
two 18.2 cm x 180 cm (7^1/$_4$ in x 71 in) strips for the outer borders;
two 18.2 cm x 149 cm (7^1/$_4$ in x 59^1/$_2$) strips for the outer borders.

Note that seam allowances of 6 mm (^{1}/$_4$ in) are included in these measurements. First attach the inner dark green borders, then the chevron borders and, finally, the dark green outer border. Use the quilt photograph as a guide.

ASSEMBLING

STEP ONE

Cut the backing fabric into two 1.6 m (1^3/$_4$ yd) lengths. Remove the selvages, then rejoin the pieces to form the complete backing, 1.6 m x 2.2 m (1^3/$_4$ yd x 2^1/$_2$ yd).

STEP TWO

Place the backing fabric, face down, on the floor or a large table. Secure it with pins or tape. Place the wadding and quilt top (face up) in the centre of the backing fabric. Secure the layers of the quilt sandwich with basting or safety pins. Bring the excess backing fabric to the front of the quilt and baste it over the raw edges to protect them during quilting.

STEP THREE

Transfer the quilting design from template D to the small green squares.

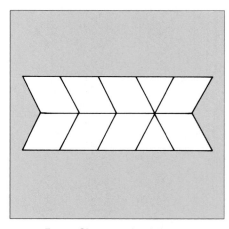

Fig. 1: Changing the direction of the chevrons

QUILTING

Using the green quilting thread and quilting needle, quilt 'in-the-ditch' (along seam lines) for each block in the pieced centre and each chevron. Quilt parallel lines, approximately 3 cm (1$\frac{1}{4}$ in) apart, along the length of the dark green borders or quilt a pattern of your choice. Quilt the pattern into the green squares at the corners of the chevron border.

FINISHING

STEP ONE

Carefully trim the wadding and the backing to the size of the quilt top.

STEP TWO

Cut 9 cm (3$\frac{1}{2}$ in) wide strips from the dark green fabric down the length of the fabric for the binding. You will need two pieces approximately 220 cm (86$\frac{1}{2}$ in) long and two pieces approximately 149 cm (58$\frac{1}{2}$ in). Press the strips over double. Machine-stitch the binding to the right side of the quilt with the raw edges matching. Stitch the long sides first. Stitch the top and bottom binding, allowing 12 mm ($\frac{1}{2}$ in) to extend beyond the quilt on both ends. Turn the folded edge of this binding to the back of the quilt and slipstitch all the binding in place. At each corner tuck in the excess binding to cover the raw edges.

Don't forget to sign and date your quilt.

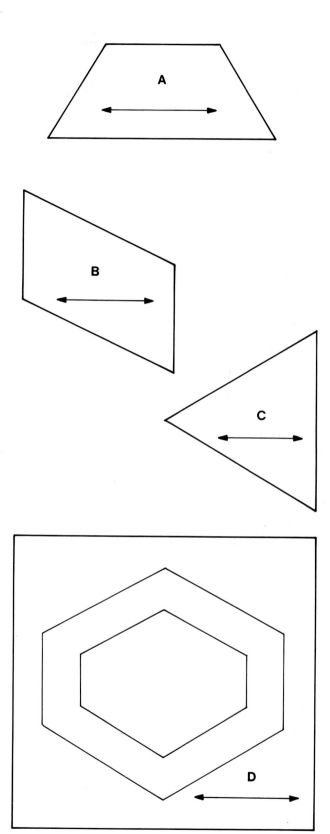

WOOL PICNIC RUG

By Jenny Seymour

With an unexpected supply of tailor's suiting samples, I decided to re-create a wool quilt like those made during the Depression. With resources so scarce then, the backing of these makeshift coverings was often made from bags sewn together. This wool picnic rug is backed with fleecy cotton, a cosy and much more attractive alternative to sacking.

FINISHED SIZE

Quilt: 125 cm (50 in) square
Block size: 25 cm (10 in) square
Total number of blocks: thirteen plain blocks and twelve pieced blocks

Machine-pieced and machine-quilted

FABRIC SUGGESTIONS

Wool, recycled denim and corduroy would all be quite suitable. You may be able to find an interesting collection of wool pieces from secondhand clothing shops or, if you are very lucky, you may have access to a collection of samples.

FABRIC QUANTITIES

Large scraps of wool for the 25 cm (10 in) squares (a total of 1.2 m (1$^1/_3$ yd))
Smaller scraps of wool (a total of 1.2 m (1$^1/_3$ yd))
170 cm (68 in) of fabric for the backing
50 cm (20 in) of fabric for the binding

NOTIONS

Large sheet of graph paper
Glass-headed pins
Rotary cutter, board and square ruler (optional)
Paper for the templates
Pencil and ruler
Matching sewing thread (medium grey will blend with most fabrics)
Sewing machine

MAKING TEMPLATES AND CUTTING

See the template on page 16.
Due to the special requirements of working with wool, you will need to make templates from paper following the solid lines, then pin them to the fabric before cutting around them. The seam allowance of 6 mm ($^1/_4$ in) is included in the template. If you are working with other lighter fabrics, such as cottons or denims, make a template with no seam allowance, following the broken line.

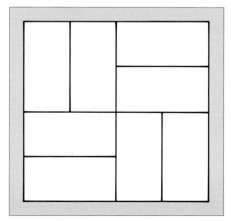

Block diagram

STEP ONE

Cut out a 26.2 cm (10$^1/_2$ in) square from the large sheet of graph paper. Pin it securely to the fabric and cut carefully around the outside. Cut out thirteen squares. A rotary cutter and board and a large square ruler can also be used to cut these squares.

STEP TWO

Trace the cutting line (the solid line) of the rectangular template onto paper, using the sharpened pencil and ruler to ensure the lines are straight. Cut out the template and pin it securely to the fabric. Cut out ninety-six rectangles.

PIECING

STEP ONE

Using a 6 mm ($^1/_4$ in) seam allowance, sew the rectangles together in pairs along the long side to form forty-eight squares.

STEP TWO

Make the pieced block by joining four squares as shown in the block diagram. Make twelve pieced blocks.

STEP THREE

Sew the blocks together in rows, alternating the pieced and plain blocks as shown in the photograph. Do not sew the rows together.

ASSEMBLING

STEP ONE

Cut a 110 cm x 130 cm (44 in x 52 in) piece from the backing fabric. Cut four pieces 10 cm x 66.2 cm (4 in x 26 in). Join them to form two strips, each 10 cm by 130 cm (4 in x 52 in). Join these strips to the sides of the large piece to form the backing, 130 cm x 130 cm (52 in x 52 in).

STEP TWO

To join the rows of blocks to the backing, lay the prepared backing fabric out flat with the wrong side uppermost. Pin the first row at the bottom edge of the backing, with the right side up. Place the next row on top of the first row, with the right sides together. Attach the two rows to the backing by sewing through the top edge of the first row, the bottom edge of the second row and the backing. Fold back the second row so that the right side is showing and press it flat. Continue in this manner, attaching each row in turn to the backing and the previous row.

FINISHING

STEP ONE

Trim the pieced top and backing so the edges are even. Cut five 10 cm (4 in) strips across the width of the binding fabric. Join the strips to form one long strip. Cut this into 130 cm (52 in) lengths. Fold each strip over double, with the wrong sides together.

STEP TWO

Find the centre of the binding strip and of the quilt sides by folding. Sew the binding to the right side of the quilt top with the raw edges even and the centres matching. Stitch from corner to corner, finishing with a backstitch. First attach the binding to two opposite edges of the quilt, trim. Turn the folded edge to the back of the quilt.

STEP THREE

Attach the binding to the remaining two edges in the same manner, leaving at least 12 mm ($\frac{1}{2}$ in) extending beyond the edges of the quilt. Fold this binding over to the back of the quilt and slipstitch all the binding in place. Fold in the excess on the ends of the binding to cover the raw edges.

Don't forget to sign and date your quilt.

The pieced block

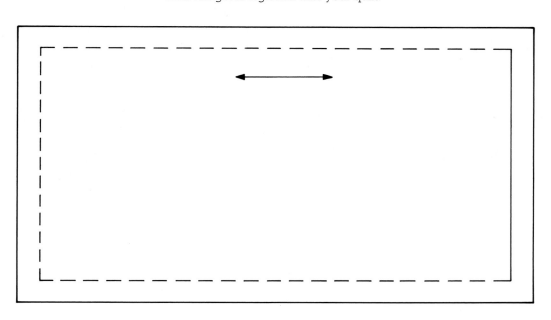

GOLDEN OLDIE

By Evelyn Seymour

The blue and brown fabric was the inspiration for the subdued colour scheme of my quilt. I really loved the fabric and decided only to use colours from it for the rest of my quilt, giving me a quilt with no strong contrasts. The fifteen large blocks went together quickly, and I enjoyed piecing the borders, which provided an interesting frame for the blocks.

FINISHED SIZE

Quilt: approximately 175 cm x 237.5 cm (70 in x 95 in)
Block size: 37.5 cm (15 in) square
Total number of blocks: fifteen

Hand-pieced and hand-quilted

FABRIC QUANTITIES

2.4 m (2²/₃ yd) of light fabric
2 m (2¹/₄ yd) of mid-blue fabric
2 m (2¹/₄ yd) of dark blue fabric
2 m (2¹/₄ yd) of blue/brown fabric
3.5 m (3⁷/₈ yd) of brown fabric
188 cm x 250 cm (74 in x 100 in) of wadding
5 m (5⁵/₈ yd) of fabric for the backing

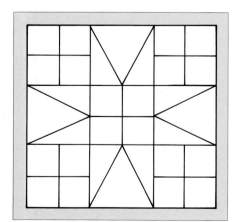

Block diagram

NOTIONS

Template plastic
Fineline permanent marker pen
Glass-headed pins
Pencil, B
Pencil for marking dark fabric, silver or yellow
Matching sewing thread
Ecru quilting thread
Fabric scissors
Paper scissors
Sheet of paper
Safety pins
Craft knife
Betweens needles, size 9 or 10, for piecing and quilting
Long thin needle for basting
'Quilters Quarter' or 6 mm (¹/₄ in) wide masking tape for marking the quilting lines
Plastic bags
Quilting hoop or frame
Masking tape
Chalk dispenser

MAKING TEMPLATES

See the templates and the quilting pattern on pages 21-23. Note that the templates do not include seam allowances. Trace the templates A, B, C, D and E onto the template plastic. Use a ruler for drawing the long straight lines. Mark the grain line on each template, then carefully cut them out.

CUTTING

All border measurements include 6 mm (¹/₄ in) seam allowances and an additional allowance of 4 cm (1¹/₂ in) for any adjustments.

STEP ONE

From the light fabric, cut two pieces 7.5 cm x 179 cm (3 in x 71¹/₂ in) and two pieces 13.7 cm x 229 cm (5¹/₂ in x 92 in) down the length of the fabric first, for the borders.

STEP TWO

From the mid-blue fabric, cut two pieces 7.5 cm x 116.5 cm (3 in x 46 in) and two pieces 7.5 cm x 191 cm (3 in x 76 in) along the length of the fabric first, for the borders.

Detail of part of the block, showing the quilting pattern

STEP THREE

From the dark blue fabric, cut five 9 cm (3½ in) wide strips down the length of the fabric for the binding.

STEP FOUR

You will need to work on a large flat surface to mark out the fabric because of the large templates. You may find it helpful to use a ruler here to ensure accuracy in marking out the long straight edges.

On the wrong side of the fabric, carefully trace around the required number of pieces for each shape leaving space between each one to allow for seams. These pencil lines will be your sewing lines. Cut out each piece approximately 6 mm (¼ in) from the sewing line.

Cut out the following pieces:
From the light fabric, one hundred and twenty A;
from the mid-blue fabric, ninety A;
from the dark blue fabric, ninety A;
from the brown fabric, sixty B, sixteen C, forty-four E;
from the blue/brown fabric, twenty-six D and one hundred and twenty C.
Place the different shapes in separate plastic bags for ease of use.

PIECING

STEP ONE

Assemble the required pieces for each block: eight A in light fabric, six A in dark blue fabric, six A in mid-blue fabric, eight C in blue/brown fabric, four B in brown fabric. Following the block diagram, place the pieces in position on the large sheet of paper. Secure each piece with a single pin.

STEP TWO

Following figure 1, sew the pieces together into nine small units, then join them into three rows of three. Complete the block by joining the rows together. Make fifteen blocks.

STEP THREE

Sew the blocks together in five rows of three blocks each.

FOR THE INNER BORDER

STEP ONE

Attach two 7.5 cm x 116.5 cm (3 in x 46 in) mid-blue strips to the top and bottom of the assembled quilt top Trim.

STEP TWO

Measure between the two attached strips. Trim the remaining mid-blue strips to this measurement plus 12 mm (½ in) for seam allowances. Attach a dark blue A to one end of the two strips of mid-blue. Attach a mid-blue square to the other end of the strips. Join these to either side of the assembled blocks. Make sure the small squares are exactly at the corner and that the dark blue squares line up with the diagonal rows of dark squares in the quilt top.

FOR THE PIECED BORDER

STEP ONE

Using five D pieces in blue/brown fabric, eight E pieces in brown fabric and four C pieces in brown fabric, assemble the short pieced border as shown in figure 2. Make another one the same.

STEP TWO

Using eight D pieces in blue/brown fabric, fourteen E pieces in brown fabric and four C pieces in brown fabric, assemble the long pieced border as shown in figure 3. Make another one the same.

STEP THREE

Make four 4-patch blocks, using two A pieces in dark blue and two A pieces in mid-blue. Attach one to either end of the short pieced borders as indicated in figure 2.

STEP FOUR

Attach the long borders to the sides of the quilt top, then attach the short borders to the top and bottom.

FOR THE OUTER BORDER

Attach two 13.7 cm x 229 cm (5½ in x 92 in) pieces to either side of the quilt top. Attach two 7.5 cm x 179 cm (3 in x 71½ in) strips cut from the light fabric to the top and bottom of the quilt top.

The pieced and quilted borders

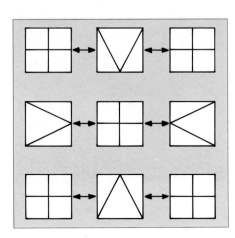

Fig. 1: Piecing the block

ASSEMBLING

STEP ONE

Trace the quilting pattern from page 23 onto the template plastic. Using the craft knife, cut a stencil from the pattern, ensuring that the cuts are wide enough to enable you to draw through them with a pencil. Using this quilting pattern or one of your own, mark the quilt top using a pencil or chalk dispenser. For ease of marking the grid lines, make a strip 1.5 cm ($^5/_8$ in) wide from strong cardboard, approximately 30 cm (12 in) long. You will find using 6 mm ($^1/_4$ in) wide masking tape or a 'Quilters Quarter' invaluable when you need to mark lines that are 6 mm ($^1/_4$ in) apart.

STEP TWO

Cut the backing fabric in half, giving two 2.5 m ($2^3/_4$ yd) pieces. Remove the selvages, then rejoin the pieces to form the complete backing 2.2 m x 2.5 m ($2^1/_3$ yd x $2^3/_4$ yd).

STEP THREE

Place the backing face down on the floor or a large table. Anchor the backing fabric to the floor with safety pins (in the case of carpet) or with tape to make sure it is perfectly flat. Place the wadding and quilt top, face up, in the centre of the backing fabric. Smooth out each layer as it is put down. When you are satisfied that your quilt sandwich is perfectly flat, secure the three layers together with safety pins or with basting. Roll the excess backing onto the front to protect the wadding during quilting.

QUILTING

STEP ONE

Using the ecru quilting thread and the size 9 or 10 quilting needle, hand-quilt the entire quilt. You will need to use a hoop to ensure that the three layers remain flat. If you have used safety pins to secure the three layers, then you may find you need to move one or two from time to time if they get in the way of the hoop.

STEP TWO

To complete the quilting on the borders, undo the folded excess border fabric. A square quilting frame will facilitate quilting of the borders.

FINISHING

STEP ONE

Carefully trim the wadding and the backing to the size of the quilt top.

STEP TWO

Join 9 cm ($3^1/_2$ in) wide strips of dark blue fabric to form two 179 cm ($71^1/_2$ in) long strips and two 242 cm (95 in) long strips for the binding. Find the centre of the binding strips and of the quilt sides by folding. Press the strips over double. Machine-stitch the binding to the right side of the quilt with the raw edges even and the centres matching. Stitch the long sides first. Turn the folded edge of the binding to the back of the quilt.

STEP THREE

Stitch the top and bottom binding allowing 2 cm ($^3/_4$ in) to extend beyond the quilt at both ends. Turn the folded edge of this binding to the back of the quilt. Slipstitch all the binding into place, folding in the excess binding to cover the raw edges.

Don't forget to sign and date your quilt.

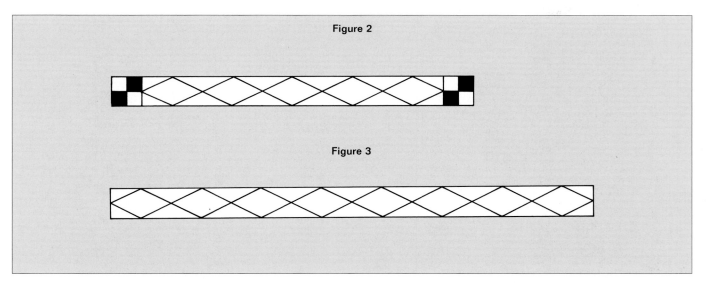

Fig. 2: Piecing the short border   Fig.3. Piecing the long border

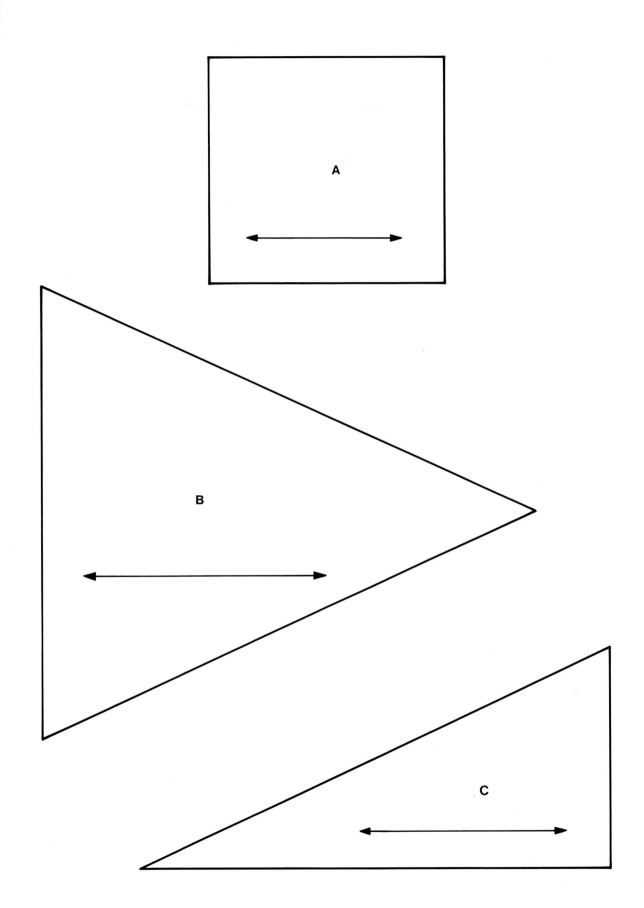

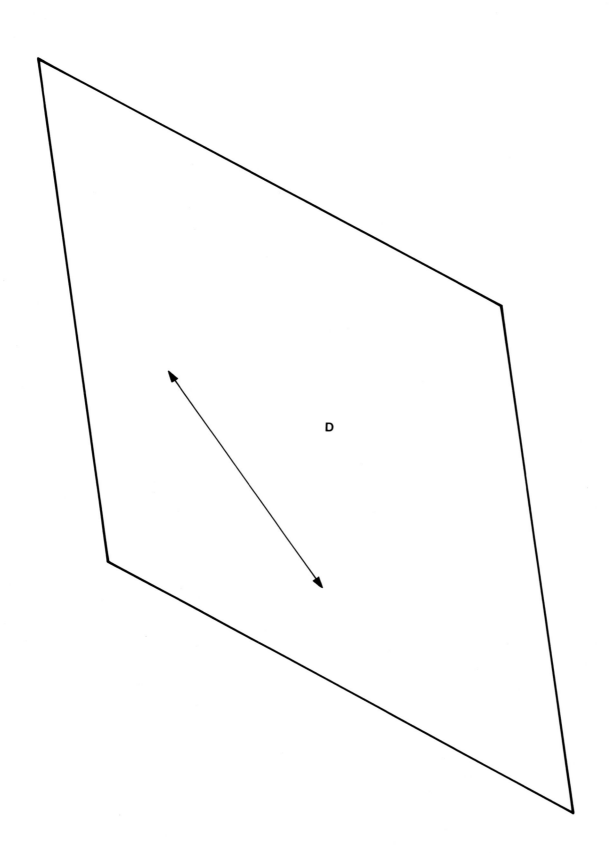

D

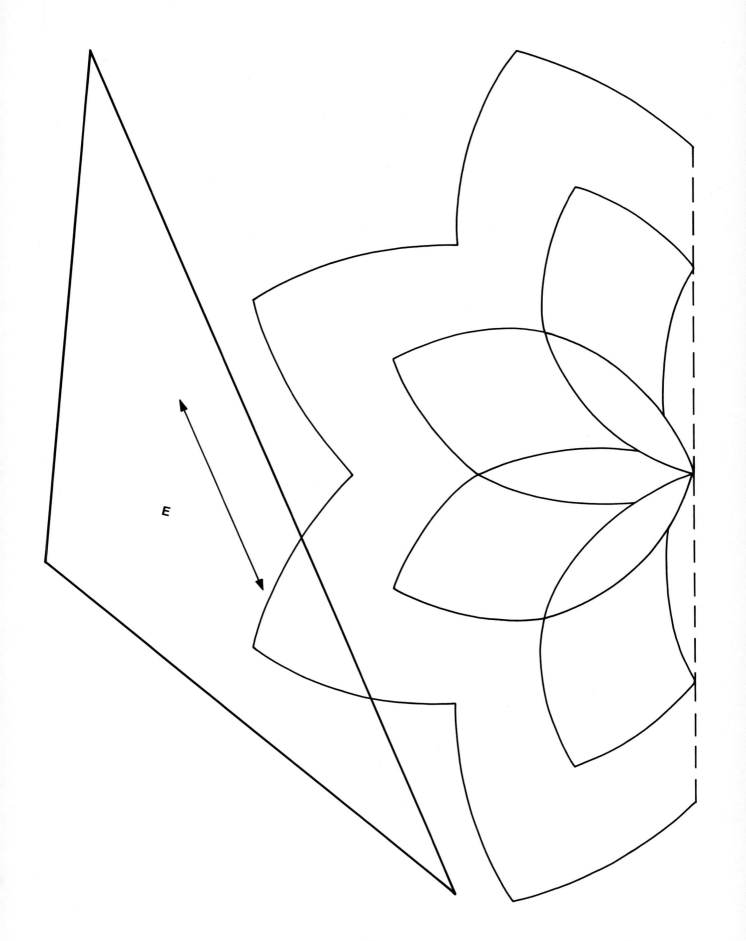

E

TRIBUTE TO TRALEE

By Sue Manchip

This was my very first experience with friendship quilts and I chose a simple nine-patch to evoke memories of friendship quilts of the past. Having chosen the Single Irish Chain pattern, I named the quilt as a link to my grandfather's home town in Ireland – Tralee. The quilting pattern features hearts, symbolising my friendship with the Mirrabooka Quilters.

FINISHED SIZE

Quilt: 192 cm x 234 cm (81 in x 99 in)
Block size: 21 cm (9 in) square
Total number of blocks: thirty-two pieced blocks arranged with thirty-one plain blocks in a checkerboard pattern.
NOTE: In this quilt, the conversion from metric to imperial measurements is not exact, as the nine-patch block is best attempted using a measurement divisible by three. If you are using imperial measurements you will need to draw a 3 in square for the template.

Hand-pieced and hand-quilted

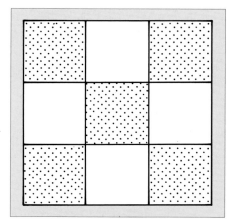

Block diagram

FABRIC QUANTITIES

10 cm (4 in) each of twenty different blue fabrics
Scraps of another twelve other different blue fabrics
5 m (5$\frac{1}{2}$ yd) of white fabric
2.1 m (2$\frac{3}{8}$ yd) of blue print fabric for the border
4.8 m (5$\frac{3}{4}$ yd) of fabric for the backing
1 m (1$\frac{1}{8}$ yd) of blue fabric for the binding

NOTIONS

Template plastic
Heavy cardboard or rotary cutter and square ruler
Fineline permanent marker pen
Sandpaper board
Architect's tracing paper
Felt-tip pen
Large sheet of paper
Pencil, B
Matching sewing thread
Fabric scissors
Paper scissors
Quilting thread, white
Betweens needles, size 9 or 10, for piecing and quilting
Long thin needle for basting or safety pins (approximately 450)
Quilting hoop

MAKING TEMPLATES

See the template and the quilting pattern on pages 27 and 28. Note that the template does not include seam allowances.

Trace the template onto the template plastic, using the marker pen or pencil. Mark the grain line on the template, then cut it out, using the paper scissors.

CUTTING

STEP ONE

To cut out, place the fabric face down on the sandpaper board. Place the template on the wrong side of the fabric, matching the grain line of the fabric and the marked grain line on the template. Trace carefully around the template with the pencil, leaving space between each shape to allow for seams. This pencil line will be your sewing line. Cut out each piece approximately 6 mm ($\frac{1}{4}$ in) from the sewing line. Cut out the following pieces: six A from each of four of the blue fabrics, ten A from each of ten of the blue fabrics, nine A from each of six of the blue fabrics, and one A from each of the twelve blue scraps.

From the white fabric, cut two pieces 9 cm x 193 cm (3½ in x 82 ½ in) and two pieces 9 cm x 166 cm (3½ in x 70 in) down the length of the fabric for the inner border.

From the blue print border fabric, cut two pieces 16.2 cm x 208 cm (6½ in x 88½ in) and two pieces 16.2 cm x 196 cm (6½ in x 82½ in). Measurements for the borders include seam allowances plus an additional allowance of 4 cm (1½ in) in length for adjustments.

STEP THREE

For the plain squares, make a template from heavy cardboard that is a 21 cm (9 in) square. Mark thirty squares on the white fabric, leaving at least 12 mm (½ in) between them. Cut out each square approximately 6 mm (¼ in) from the sewing line. Alternatively, cut thirty 22.2 cm (9½ in) squares using a rotary cutter and square ruler. Note that seam allowances are included in these measurements for rotary cutting.

STEP FOUR

Cut one hundred and twenty-eight A from the white fabric.

PIECING

STEP ONE

Twenty blocks are pieced using four white squares and five blue squares of the same blue fabric. Twelve blocks are pieced using four white squares and five different blues. The blues used in these twelve blocks should match the blue used in the diagonally adjoining block. This is apparent when you study the detail of the quilt. The blue centres in these blocks are those cut from scraps. Pin the pieces required for one block onto the large sheet of paper.

STEP TWO

Using the photographs and the block diagram as a guide, sew three squares together to form a row, then join three rows to complete the block.

STEP THREE

Join the completed blocks with the large white squares in rows to form a checkerboard. Be careful to place the pieced squares so that the fabric used in the corners of diagonally adjacent blocks is the same.

FOR THE INNER BORDER

Attach the long white border strips to both sides of the quilt top, then attach the remaining strips to the top and bottom of the quilt top.

FOR THE OUTER BORDER

Attach the 16.2 cm x 208 cm (6½ in x 88½ in) blue print strips to the sides of the quilt top. Attach the 16.2 cm x 196 cm (6½ in x 82½ in) blue print strips to top and bottom of the quilt top.

ASSEMBLING

STEP ONE

Trace the quilting patterns onto the architect's tracing paper, then outline the designs with the felt-tip pen. Place the large heart design under each large white square and trace the design onto the fabric using the pencil, pressing lightly. Trace the line of hearts onto the white borders in the same way.

STEP TWO

Cut the backing fabric in half to give two 2.4 m (2⅞ yd) lengths. Remove the selvages, then rejoin the pieces to give the backing piece, 2.2 m x 2.4 m (2½ yd x 2⅞ yd).

STEP THREE

Place the backing fabric face down with the wadding on top, then the quilt top, face up, on top of that, smoothing each layer as it is put down. Keeping the three layers as flat as possible, pin them together at about 10 cm (4 in) intervals with safety pins or baste the quilt sandwich. For tips on basting the quilt sandwich, see page 77.

QUILTING

Using the white quilting thread, the quilting needles and the quilting hoop, hand-quilt the entire quilt in the marked patterns.

FINISHING

STEP ONE

Carefully trim the wadding and the backing to the size of the quilt top. Cut the binding fabric into 9 cm (3½ in) wide strips across the width of the fabric. Join them to form two 238 cm (101 in) long strips and two 196 cm (83 in) long strips for the binding.

Detail of the large heart quilting pattern

STEP TWO

Press each strip over double. Machine-stitch the binding to the right side of the quilt with the raw edges even. Stitch the long sides first. Turn the folded edge of the binding to the back of the quilt.

STEP THREE

Stitch the top and bottom binding, allowing at least 12 mm ($\frac{1}{2}$ in) to extend beyond the quilt on both sides. Turn the folded edge of this binding to the back of the quilt. Slipstitch all the binding in place. At each corner fold the excess fabric to cover the raw edges.

Don't forget to sign and date your quilt.

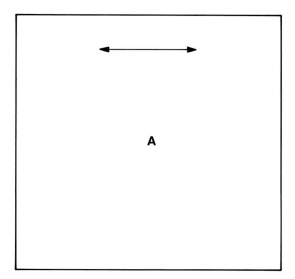

A

Large Heart Quilting Pattern

HEARTS AND FLOWERS

By Ros Stinson

I wanted to use all my favourite pink and blue print fabrics to make a pretty quilt for my niece Jessica who always enjoys sleeping under a quilt when she comes to stay. My selection of fabrics allows the quilt to be 'quietly scrappy' while the two different quilted grids enhance the design. Jessica loves the pink and blue hearts.

FINISHED SIZE

Quilt: 160 cm x 200 cm (64 in x 80 in)
Block size: 40 cm (16 in) square
Total number of blocks: twelve

Hand-pieced and hand-quilted

FABRIC QUANTITIES

20 cm (8 in) each of fifteen medium blue fabrics, fifteen medium pink fabrics, and fifteen light blue/pink fabrics
4 m (4½ yd) of white fabric
2 m (2¼ yd) of blue-and-white fabric for the outer border
1.9 m (2⅛ yd) of blue fabric for the inner border
4.4 m (4⅞ yd) of pink fabric for the binding and the backing (a light colour or white is best to avoid any show-through)
170 cm x 210 cm (68 in x 84 in) of wadding

NOTIONS

Template plastic
Fineline permanent marker pen
Sandpaper board
Thin cardboard for appliqué
Pencil, B
Matching sewing thread
Quilting thread, white
Fabric scissors
Paper scissors
Glass-headed pins
Long thin needle for basting
Quilting hoop
Betweens needles, size 9 or 10, for piecing and quilting
6 mm (¼ in) wide masking tape
Spray starch
Craft knife

MAKING TEMPLATES

See the templates and quilting patterns on pages 32-34 and the inner border quilting pattern on the Pull Out Pattern Sheet. Note that the templates do not include seam allowances.

Using the marker pen, trace the templates A, B, C, D, E, F and G onto the template plastic. Trace template B a second time, cut it out, turn it over and mark it Br. Mark the grain line on each template. Cut each template out carefully.

CUTTING

STEP ONE

The measurements for the borders and bindings include 6 mm (¼ in) seam allowances. From the blue inner border fabric, cut two 9.2 cm x 146 cm (3¾ in x 58 in) pieces and two 9.2 cm x 182 cm (3¾ in x 73 in) pieces. Use the remainder as one of the blue fabrics in the blocks.

STEP TWO

From the blue and white print fabric for the outer border, cut two pieces 13.2 cm x 210 cm (5¼ in x 84 in) and two pieces 13.2 cm x 170 cm (5¼ in x 67 in) down the length of the fabric. (Note that 10 cm (4 in) has been added to the required border length to allow

Block diagram

The quilting features hearts and flowers

for the mitred corner). Use the remaining fabric for one of the blue fabrics in the blocks.

STEP THREE

From the pink fabric, cut eight 9 cm x 110 cm ($3^{1}/_{2}$ in x 44 in) across the width of the fabric for the binding. The remaining piece is for the backing.

STEP FOUR

From the white fabric, cut forty-eight D, ninety-six C, forty-eight A and twelve E.

STEP FIVE

Place the templates on the wrong side of the fabrics and draw around them with the pencil. This pencil line will be your sewing line. When marking fabric for the blocks, leave space between each shape to allow for seams. Cut out each piece approximately 6 mm ($^{1}/_{4}$ in) from the sewing line.

For each block you will need four D, eight C, four A and one E in white; four B from each of two blue, pink or light fabrics; four Br from each of two blue, pink or light fabrics; twelve C in assorted fabrics, different from those already used for the block; and one F using pink or blue fabric. Mark the sewing line on the right side of the fabric for F and allow 12 mm ($^{1}/_{2}$ in) for seam allowances.

HINT: You may wish to cut out all the white pieces first and only cut out the patterned pieces when you are ready to start a new block. That way you can make sure there is a balance in the use of the pink and blue fabrics.

PIECING

STEP ONE

Cut out one F in thin cardboard. Attach the fabric F to the cardboard by turning the seam allowance over the cardboard and basting it in place. Spray with a little starch, press, then remove

the cardboard. Because this is a large piece to appliqué, you may want to dispense with the cardboard template and simply turn under and baste the seam allowance to the back. Cut the central V almost to the sewing line to facilitate either method.

STEP TWO

Find the centre of the large white square E by folding it into quarters. Finger-press the folds. Fold the heart in half vertically to find the centre. Appliqué the heart to the white square, matching the centre lines and using blue or pink thread as appropriate.

STEP THREE

Assemble the block following figure 1. Make twelve blocks.

STEP FOUR

Sew the blocks together in three rows of four blocks each.

FOR THE INNER BORDER

Find the centre of the border strips and of the sides of the pieced top by folding. Using the inner border strips already cut from the blue fabric and matching centres, attach the short strips to the top and bottom of the quilt, then attach the longer strips to sides of the quilt top. Mitre the corners. Trim the seams and press.

Fig. 1: The piecing diagram

FOR THE OUTER BORDER

Using the blue and white border strips already cut and matching centres, sew the short strips to the top and bottom of the quilt, then attach the long strips to the sides. Mitre the corners. Trim the seams and press.

ASSEMBLING

STEP ONE

Cut the remaining pink backing fabric into two pieces, each 170 cm (68 in) approximately long. Remove the selvages, then rejoin the pieces to form a backing 170 cm x 220 cm (68 in x 88 in).

STEP TWO

Following the quilting patterns indicated on the templates, mark the quilt top using the pencil or you can use your own pattern, if you prefer. The diagonally gridded lines are called cross-hatching. To make the cross-hatching easier, cut strips from template plastic, 1 cm ($^{3}/_{8}$ in) and 2.5 cm (1 in) wide and approximately 20 cm (8 in) long. Use these to mark the cross-hatching: the large square with 2.5 cm (1 in) cross-hatching and the small square and heart with 1 cm ($^{3}/_{8}$ in) cross-hatching.

STEP THREE

Mark the small heart quilting pattern onto the appliqué heart and the white square. The same pattern is also overlapped, on the outer border. Placement of the design is clearly shown in the photograph of the quilt.

STEP FOUR

Trace the inner border quilting pattern onto the template plastic and make your own stencil using a craft knife. Cut along the lines, making a cut wide enough for a pencil to fit. The flower in this design is also used in the small white squares and white triangles in the block. Again, refer to the photographs for a guide.

STEP FIVE

Place the backing fabric face down on a table or on the floor and secure it with pins or tape. Place the wadding on top, then the quilt top on top of that, face upwards. Smooth out each layer as it is put down. When all the layers are perfectly flat, baste them together, rolling the backing onto the front and basting it over the raw edges to protect them during quilting.

QUILTING

Using the white quilting thread, quilting needle and hoop, hand-quilt the entire quilt, beginning at the centre and working out towards the edges.

The back of the quilt shows off the beautiful hand-quilting

FINISHING

STEP ONE

Carefully trim the wadding and the backing to the size of the quilt top.

STEP TWO

Join the pink binding strips, already cut, to form two strips 204 cm (81 in) and two strips 164 cm (65 in) long. Press the strips over double. Find the centres as for the borders. Machine-stitch them to the right side of the quilt with the raw edges even and the centres matching. Sew the long strips to the sides first. Turn the folded edge of the binding to the wrong side of the quilt. Stitch the remaining strips to the top and bottom. Note that there is at least 12 mm ($^{1}/_{2}$ in) overhang at either end of the binding strips. Turn this binding to the back of the quilt and slipstitch all the binding in place, folding in the excess binding to cover the raw edges.

Don't forget to sign and date your quilt.

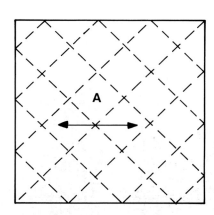

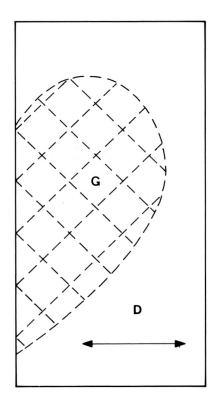

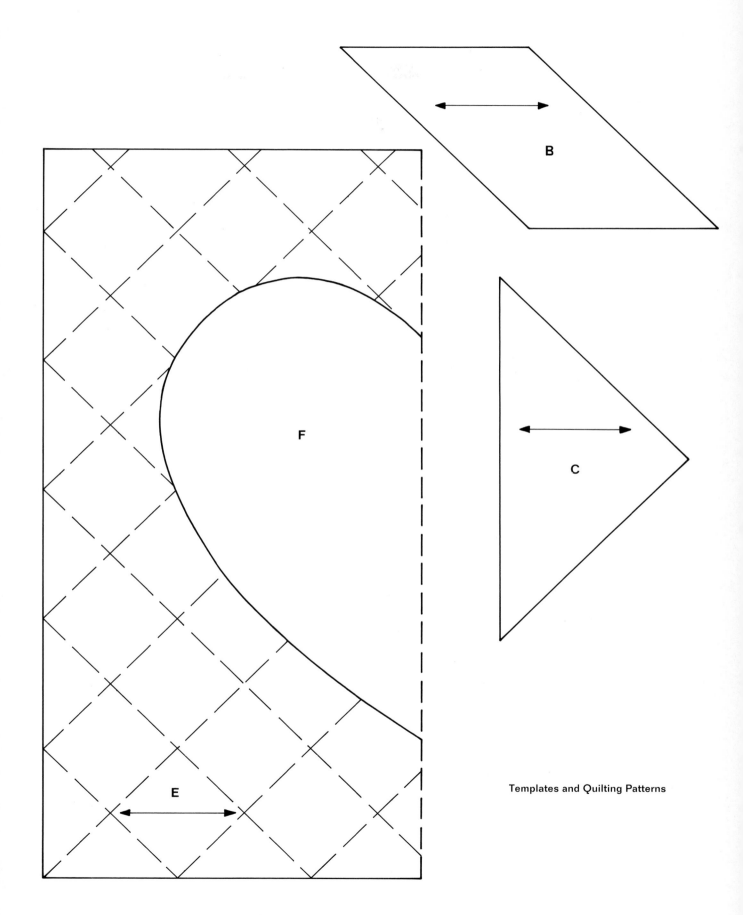

B

C

E

F

Templates and Quilting Patterns

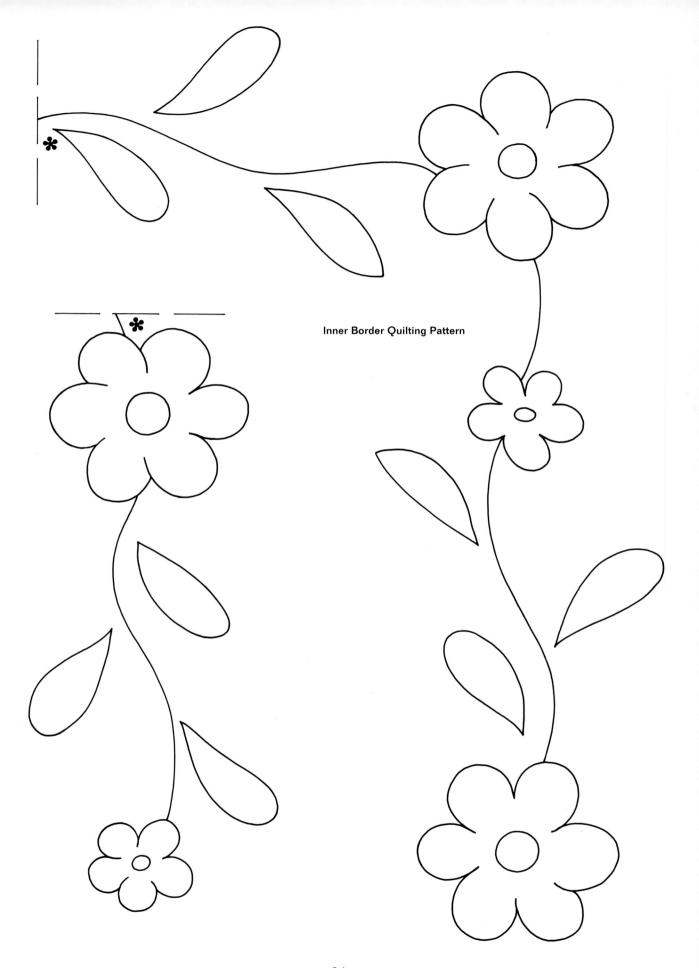

Inner Border Quilting Pattern

MEMORIES

By Evelyn Seymour

Yellow has always been a difficult colour for me to include in my quilts. However, when I found this wonderful yellow fabric, I determined to pick up the challenge and make it work in one of my quilts. In fact, the yellow became the unifying factor in this scrap quilt. I chose the quilting design to emphasise the optical illusion of curves created by straight lines.

FINISHED SIZE

Quilt: 100 cm x 132 cm (36½ in x 49½ in)
Block size: 12 cm (4½ in)
Total number of blocks: thirty-five
NOTE: The imperial measurements given for this quilt are not exact conversions but are based on using a 4½ in block which is a convenient size to use.

Hand-pieced and hand-quilted

FABRIC REQUIREMENTS

Large variety of soft-toned scraps
Large variety of bright coloured scraps
70 cm (28 in) of white fabric for the triangles
50 cm (20 in) of blue fabric for the binding
1.4 m (1⅝ yd) of fabric for the backing
1.5 m (1⅔ yd) of yellow and blue print fabric for the border and pieced sashing
20 cm (8 in) of yellow spot fabric for the sashing
20 cm (8 in) of yellow swirl fabric for the centre of the Maltese cross
105 cm x 140 cm (41½ in x 55 in) of wadding

NOTIONS

Template plastic
Fineline permanent marker pen
Sandpaper board
Pencil, B
Matching sewing thread (a mid-grey is good when there are lots of fabrics to match)
Fabric scissors
Paper scissors
Quilting thread, cream
Glass-headed pins
Quilting hoop or frame
Betweens needles, size 9 or 10, for piecing and quilting
Safety pins (optional)
6 mm (¼ in) wide masking tape

MAKING TEMPLATES

See the templates on page 39. Note that the templates do not include seam allowances.

Trace templates A, B, C, D, and E onto the template plastic, using the marker pen. Mark the grain line on each template, then cut them out carefully.

CUTTING

STEP ONE

Place the fabric face down on the sandpaper board and trace around the appropriate template with the pencil. This pencil line will be your sewing

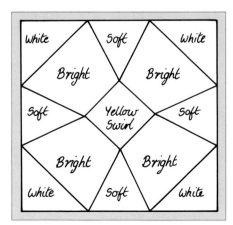

Block diagram

Four blocks separated by sashing

line. When marking the fabric, leave a space between each shape to allow for seams. Cut out each piece approximately 6 mm (^{1}/$_4$ in) from the sewing line.

STEP TWO

From the yellow and blue print fabric, cut two 9.2 cm x 110 cm (3^1/$_2$ in x 41 in) and two 9.2 cm x 142 cm (3^1/$_2$ in x 53^1/$_2$ in) pieces for the borders. Seam allowances of 6 mm (^{1}/$_4$ in) are included in these measurements as is an added 10 cm (4 in) in the length to allow for mitred corners.

STEP THREE

Cut one hundred and sixty-four E for the sashing and eighty-two E in soft-toned scraps for eighty-two sashing strips. Cut forty-eight E in the yellow spot fabric for joining the sashing strips

STEP FOUR

For each of thirty-five blocks, cut the following pieces: four B, using one of the bright coloured scraps; one A from the yellow swirl fabric, for the centre; four D from the white fabric; and four C from the soft-toned scraps, all different.

PIECING

STEP ONE

Following the piecing diagram in figure 1 and the block diagram, complete thirty-five blocks. Following figure 2, make eighty-two sashing strips.

STEP TWO

Sew the sashing strips into rows, alternating them with a yellow spot square E and beginning and ending with a yellow spot square. Use five sashing strips and six squares for each sashing row. Make eight sashing rows.

STEP THREE

Alternating sashing strips and blocks, join a block row, using five blocks and six sashing strips. Make seven block rows.

STEP FOUR

Complete the pieced quilt top by sewing sashing rows and block rows together, alternately, using the photograph as a guide. Begin with a sashing row.

FOR THE BORDER

Attach the short border pieces to the ends of the pieced top, finishing sewing at the seam line. Attach the long border pieces to the sides of the quilt top, mitring the corners. Trim any excess fabric and press the mitre seam flat.

ASSEMBLING

Lay the backing fabric face down with the wadding on top. Place the pieced top on top of that, face upwards. Smooth out each layer as you put it down. When all layers are perfectly flat, baste them together (or secure them with safety pins). Roll the excess backing to the front of the quilt and baste it in place to protect the edges during quilting.

QUILTING

Using the quilting thread and hoop or frame, hand-quilt the entire quilt following the guidelines given in figure 3, or use a design of your own choosing. Use the 6 mm (^{1}/$_4$ in) wide masking tape to mark out the design, The border is quilted, following the pattern in the fabric.

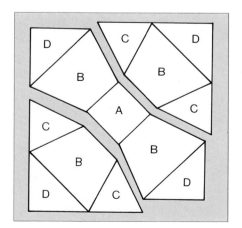

Fig. 1: The piecing diagram

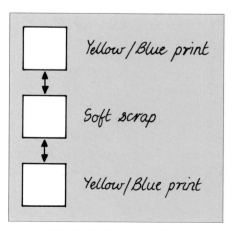

Fig. 2: Piecing the sashing

FINISHING

STEP ONE

Carefully trim the wadding and backing to the size of the quilt top.

STEP TWO

Cut binding fabric into 9 cm (3¹/₂ in) wide strips across the width of the fabric. Join the strips to form two 140 cm (55 in) and two 108 cm (42¹/₂ in) lengths. Press the strips over double.

STEP THREE

Find the centre of the binding strips and the quilt sides by folding. Machine-stitch the strips to the right side of the quilt with the raw edges even, matching the centres. Attach the short binding to the top and bottom first, then attach the long binding strips to the sides of the quilt, mitring the corners. Turn the binding to the back of the quilt and slipstitch it into place.

Don't forget to sign and date your quilt.

Evelyn has made a wonderful label for her quilt.

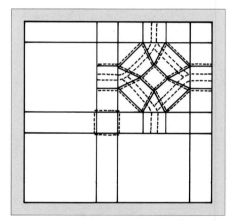

Fig. 3: The quilting design

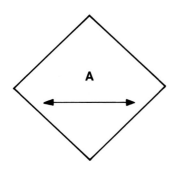

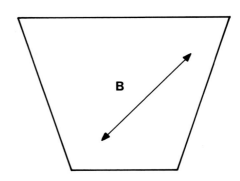

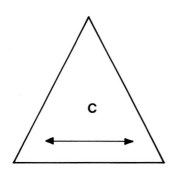

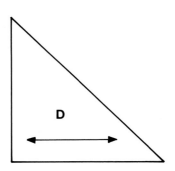

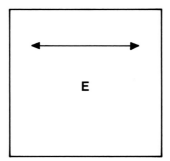

THERE'S NO PLACE LIKE HOME

By Evelyn Seymour

I love being part of quilt challenges. My quilt, 'There's No Place Like Home',
was my response to the Eastwood Patchwork Quilters' recent Black and
White Challenge which required a small quilt to be made using only black,
white and shades of grey with only one other colour to be used.
The embroidery alone took me one month to complete.

FINISHED SIZE

Quilt: 90 cm x 120 cm (35$\frac{1}{2}$ in x 47$\frac{1}{4}$ in)
Block size: various

Hand-pieced, hand-quilted and embroidered

FABRIC SUGGESTIONS

Make sure in your collection of fabrics that you include small, medium and large prints and geometric prints to provide lots of interest in the quilt. Use very dark to very light-toned fabrics to provide the contrast. This is particularly important if you are using a monochromatic colour scheme. Large scraps of fabric can also be used.

FABRIC QUANTITIES

20 cm-30 cm (8 in-12 in) black, white and all shades of grey fabrics
1.3 m (1$\frac{1}{2}$ yd) of black print fabric for the border
25 cm (10 in) of yellow fabric for the frame
Scrap of silver fabric
1.3 m (1$\frac{1}{2}$ yd) of fabric for the backing
100 cm x 130 cm (39$\frac{3}{8}$ in x 51 in) of wadding
60 cm (24 in) of black fabric for the binding

NOTIONS

Template plastic
Fineline permanent marker pen
Paper or plastic bags
Graph paper for drafting
Glass-headed pins
Drawing pins
Pencil and ruler
Sewing thread, black and grey
Quilting thread, black
Fabric scissors
Paper scissors
Quilting needles, size 9 or 10 betweens, for piecing and quilting
Long thin needle for basting
Embroidery cottons and embroidery needles
Trinkets, beads, buttons and braids
Scraps of lace, white and black

MAKING TEMPLATES

See the template for house A, the moon template S and the trees on the Pull Out Pattern Sheet. Note that the templates do not include seam allowances.

Margaret Rolfe and Beryl Hodge's book *Australian Houses in Patchwork*, published by Lothian Press, provides the other houses. Of course, you can design your own houses to fit into the spaces, the dimensions for which are given in the quilt diagram.

Trace all the templates required for houses A and trees 1 to 5, and tops 1 to 3 and the moon. As the templates are not used many times, it will be satisfactory to paste your tracing (or a photocopy) onto cardboard. Label each template, mark the grain line on each one, then cut them out carefully.

House A with embroidered detail

Embroidered garden swing and flowers

CUTTING AND PIECING

STEP ONE

Draft your own houses, church, shop on graph paper. Draft one for each space.

STEP TWO

Using the photograph and the quilt diagram as a guide, piece each block in turn, sewing smaller units together first. The blocks can all be pieced in rectangular units. Embellish them with laces and braids. As each block is completed, pin it in its correct position to a convenient wall or sheet.

STEP THREE

Cut the moon from the silver fabric. Using the grey thread, appliqué the moon onto one of the small squares S.

STEP FOUR

Assemble the quilt top, following the quilt diagram. Where possible, sew small square units together to form larger squares or rectangles. Note the position of the four small unpieced squares (template S) for appliqué or embroidery.

FOR THE YELLOW FRAME

Cut the yellow fabric into five 3 cm (1¼ in) wide strips. Join the strips end to end to form two strips 114 cm (45½ in) long and two strips 84 cm (33½ in) long. Press the strips over double with the wrong sides together, then pin them in place on the pieced quilt top with the folded edge towards the centre and the raw edges even with the edges of the quilt top.

FOR THE BORDER

Cut the black border fabric into two pieces, each 6.2 cm x 130 cm (2½ in x 52 in) and two pieces 6.2 cm x 100 cm (2½ in x 40 in). Find the centres of the border strips and of the quilt sides by folding. Attach the shorter strips to the top and bottom of the pieced quilt top, then sew the long strips to either side of the quilt, matching centres and stitching the yellow frame at the same time. Begin and end the sewing 6 mm (¼ in) from the ends. Mitre the corners of the border.

ASSEMBLING

STEP ONE

Using the photograph as a guide, add the embroidery embellishments. Do not attach any of the trinkets, beads or buttons until the quilt is finished.

STEP TWO

Place the backing fabric face down on a table, then the wadding and, finally, the quilt top, face upwards, smoothing out each layer carefully. Baste the three layers together, rolling the edges to the front and basting them in place to protect the wadding during quilting.

One of the trimmed trees

QUILTING

Using the black quilting thread and a size 9 or 10 quilting needle, hand-quilt the entire quilt. You can quilt each block in-the-ditch or let your own imagination run riot.

FINISHING

STEP ONE

Carefully trim the wadding and the backing to the size of the quilt top.

STEP TWO

Cut the binding fabric into 9 cm (3½ in) wide strips, cutting across the width of the fabric. Join the pieces to make two pieces 94 cm (37 in) long and two pieces 124 cm (48¾ in) long. Press the binding over double with the wrong sides together. Machine-stitch the binding to the right side of the quilt with the raw edges matching, stitching the binding to the sides of the quilt first. Turn the folded edge of the binding to the wrong side of the quilt.

STEP THREE

Stitch the top and bottom binding to the quilt, allowing at least 12 mm (½ in) to extend beyond the quilt on both sides. Turn the folded edge of this binding to the back of the quilt. Slipstitch all the binding into place, folding in the excess length at the ends to cover the raw edges.

STEP FOUR

Sew on the trinkets, beads and buttons.

Don't forget to sign and date your quilt.

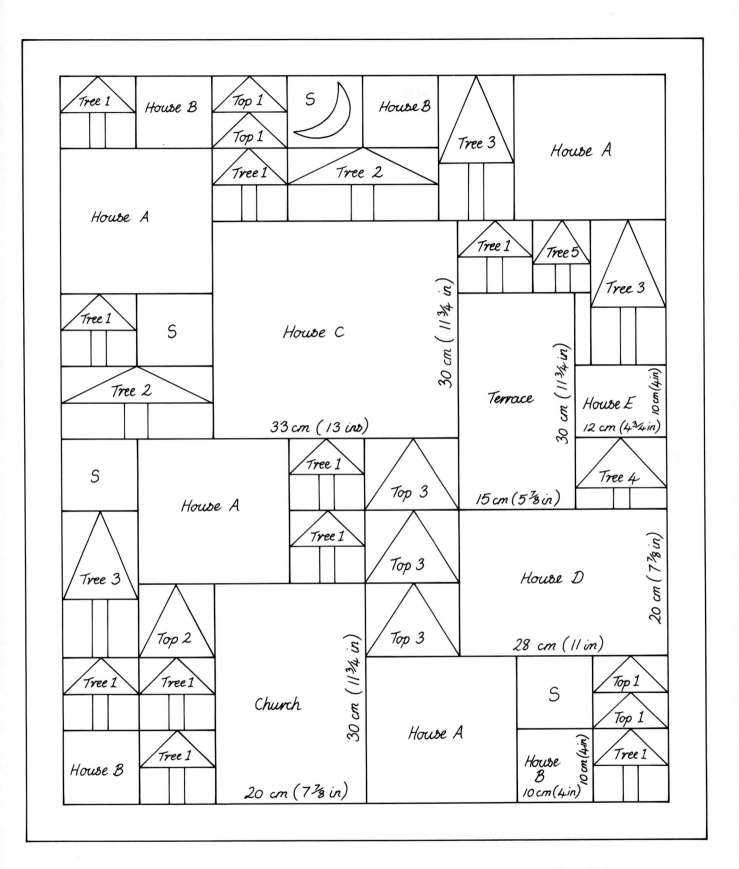

The quilt diagram

MINIATURE AMISH BASKETS

By Karen Fail

I love the look of Amish quilts. This miniature version of the Basket Quilt allowed me to experiment with the Amish palette, without the work of a large quilt. I used two purples as the backdrop for the mini-baskets, contriving the look so often achieved naturally by the Amish. The mistake in the bright pink basket is deliberate, as the Amish say 'only God is perfect'.

FINISHED SIZE

Quilt: approximately 37 cm x 45 cm (14$^1/_2$ in x 17$^3/_4$ in)
Block size: 6 cm (2$^3/_8$ in) square
Total number of blocks: twelve

Hand-pieced and hand-quilted

FABRIC QUANTITIES

Twelve different scraps of plain strong colours, one of these a lime green
10 cm (4 in) of two different shades of light and dark purple fabric
10 cm (4 in) of aqua fabric for the background in the blocks
25 cm (10 in) of black fabric
15 cm (4 in) of blue fabric for the outer border

Small piece of thin wadding, approximately 40 cm x 50 cm (16 in x 20 in)
40 cm x 50 cm (16 in x 20 in) of fabric for the backing

NOTIONS

Template plastic
Fineline permanent marker pen
Sandpaper board
Chalk dispenser
Pencil, B
Ruler
Craft knife
Pencil for marking dark fabrics, silver or yellow
Small plastic bags
Matching sewing thread
Quilting thread, black
Fabric scissors
Paper scissors

Glass-headed pins
Betweens needles, size 9 or 10, for piecing and quilting
Long thin needle for basting
Craft knife
Paper and a glue stick (optional)

MAKING TEMPLATES

See the templates and the quilting pattern on page 48. Note that the templates do not include seam allowances.

Trace the templates A, B, C, D, E, F, G, H and I onto the template plastic. Although cardboard is often used as an alternative for templates, it is essential to use template plastic for this quilt because the templates are so tiny. Mark the grain line on each one, then carefully cut out the templates.

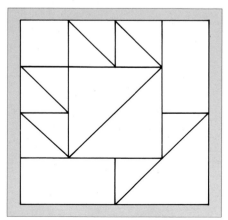

Block diagram

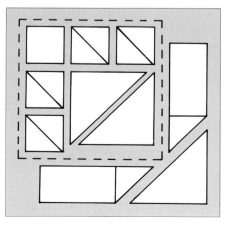

Fig. 1: The piecing diagram

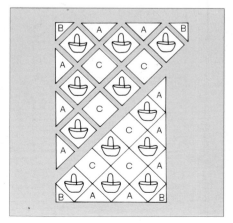

Fig. 2: Piecing the quilt top

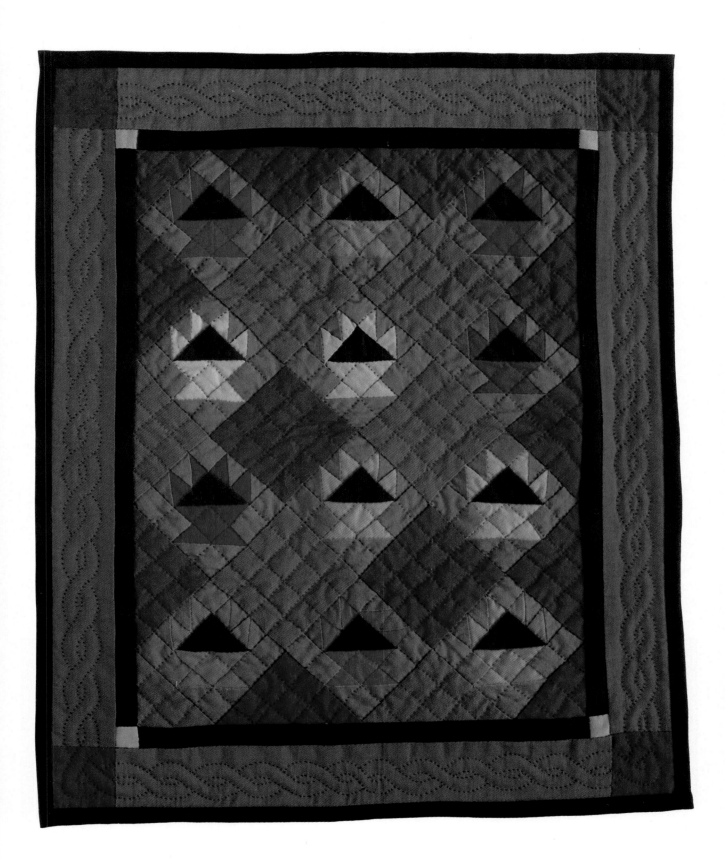

CUTTING

STEP ONE

Measurements for the borders include 6 mm ($\frac{1}{4}$ in) seam allowances. For the inner border, cut two 2.2 cm (1 in) wide strips across the width of the black fabric. Cut two 6 cm ($2\frac{3}{8}$ in) wide strips from the black fabric for the binding. For the outer border, cut two 4.7 cm ($1\frac{7}{8}$ in) wide strips across the width of the blue fabric.

STEP TWO

Place the fabric wrong side up on the sandpaper board. With the grain lines matching, carefully trace around the required number of templates for each fabric, leaving space between each shape to allow for seams. This pencil line will be your sewing line. Cut out each piece approximately 6 mm ($\frac{1}{4}$ in) from the sewing line.

Cut out the following pieces:
From the dark purple fabric, eight A, three B, two C and four I;
from the light purple fabric, two A, one B and four C;
from the aqua fabric, forty-eight D, twelve E, twenty-four F and twelve G;
from each of twelve different plains for the blocks, six D and one E;
from the black fabric, twelve E;
from the lime green fabric, cut four H.

HINT: The templates for the miniature Amish baskets are very small. As an alternative to cutting plastic templates and tracing them onto fabric, you could cut out paper templates and temporarily glue them to the fabric with a glue stick. Leave them in place until the block is sewn together, then remove them.

STEP THREE

Assemble the pieces for each block, and place them in separate small plastic bags.

PIECING

STEP ONE

Assemble the complete basket block as shown in the block diagram. Complete the square containing the basket first, then add the side pieces with the attached triangle and, finally, add the large aqua triangle to complete the block, following the piecing diagram (Fig. 1). Make twelve basket blocks, using a different plain fabric for each one. Notice the deliberate mistake in the centre bottom row.

STEP TWO

Arrange the pieced blocks, plain purple squares and triangles as shown in figure 2. Join them in diagonal rows, pressing the seams in opposite directions. It is important to carefully match the seams between the blocks.

FOR THE INNER BORDER

STEP ONE

Cut one 2.2 cm (1 in) wide strip of black fabric into two lengths, 38 cm ($15\frac{1}{4}$ in) long. Attach these strips to opposite sides of the quilt top. Trim.

STEP TWO

Measure the quilt top between the attached black strips. Use this measurement, plus 12 mm ($\frac{1}{2}$ in), to cut the remaining 2.2 cm (1 in) wide strip of black fabric into two pieces. Attach a square of light green fabric to both ends of each strip, then attach a strip to the top and bottom of the quilt top, making sure that the small green square sits exactly in the corner.

FOR THE OUTER BORDER

STEP ONE

Cut one of the 4.7 cm ($1\frac{7}{8}$ in) wide blue strips into two lengths, 42 cm ($16\frac{1}{2}$ in). Attach the strips to opposite sides of the quilt top. Trim.

STEP TWO

Measure the quilt top between the blue strips. Use this measurement, plus seam allowances of 12 mm ($\frac{1}{2}$ in), to cut the remaining 4.7 cm ($1\frac{7}{8}$ in) wide strip of blue fabric into two pieces. Attach one of the 3.5 cm ($1\frac{3}{8}$ in) purple squares to each end of the blue strips. Stitch these strips to the top and bottom of the quilt top.

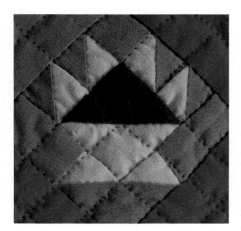

One Amish Basket

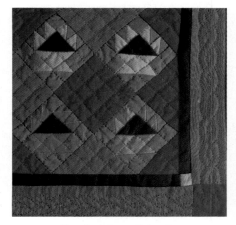

Detail of the quilt border

ASSEMBLING

STEP ONE

Using the marker pen, trace the quilting pattern onto the template plastic. Cut it out using the craft knife, being careful to remove the inner sections.

STEP TWO

Using the pencil and ruler, mark the quilt top with diagonal grid lines 1.5 cm ($^5/_8$ in) apart. Mark the quilting design along the border, beginning at the corners and working towards the middle, slightly reducing the centre loop.

STEP THREE

Lay the backing fabric face down with the wadding on top and the quilt top, face up, on top of that, smoothing out each layer as it is put down. Pin the layers together with the glass-headed pins, then baste the layers together, finishing by basting around the outside edge of the quilt.

QUILTING

Using the black quilting thread and a quilting needle, hand-quilt the entire quilt. A hoop is not required because of the small size of the quilt. For tips on hand-quilting see page 78.

FINISHING

STEP ONE

Carefully trim the wadding and the backing to the size of the quilt top.

STEP TWO

Cut two 49 cm (19 in) and two 41 cm ($16^3/_8$ in) strips from the 6 cm ($2^3/_8$ in) wide black strip. Press the strips over double. Machine-stitch the binding to the right side of the quilt with the raw edges even. Stitch the long sides first. Turn the folded edge of the binding to the wrong side of the quilt.

STEP THREE

Stitch the top and bottom bindings, allowing 12 mm ($^1/_2$ in) to extend beyond the quilt on both ends. Turn the folded edge of this binding to the back of the quilt. Slipstitch all the binding in place, folding the excess binding to cover the raw edges.

Don't forget to sign and date your quilt.

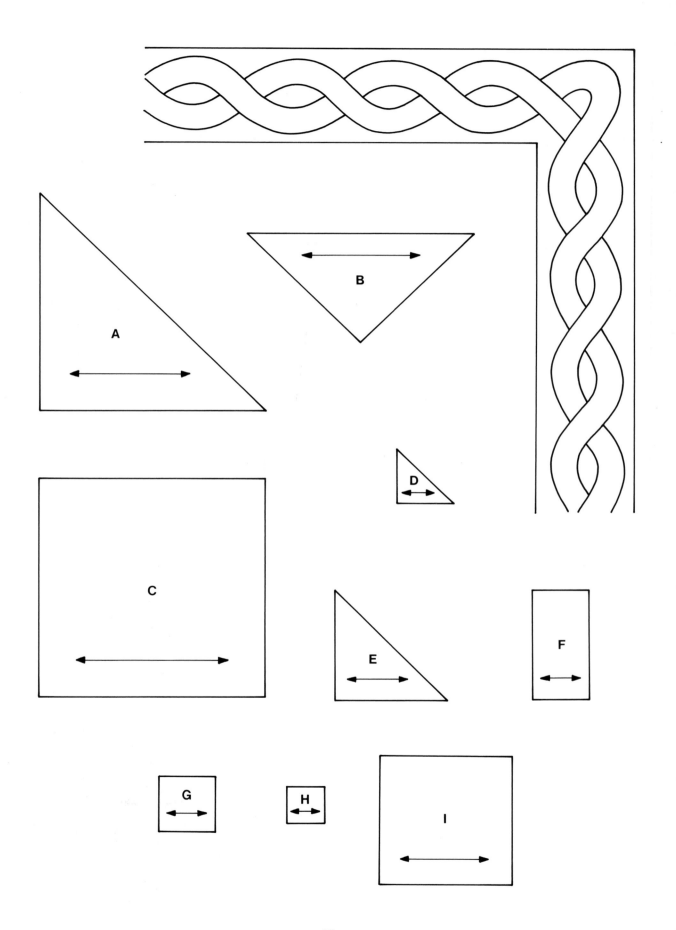

MATHEW'S SCHOOLHOUSE QUILT

By Dawn Richter

What fabrics, what pattern could I choose for a quilt for a rambunctious three-year-old? I felt I couldn't go past the Amish dark background contrasting with the stark jewel-like plains – both as protection against grubby hands, and for the sheer beauty of the combination.

FINISHED SIZE

Quilt: 206 cm x 158 cm (82$\frac{1}{2}$ in x 63 in – this is not an exact conversion, but is based on the 12 in block)
Block size: 30 cm (12 in) square
Total number of blocks: twelve

Hand-pieced and hand-quilted

FABRIC QUANTITIES

20 cm (8 in) each of twelve brightly coloured plain fabrics
4.5 m (5 yd) of black fabric
3.4 m (3$\frac{3}{4}$ yd) of backing fabric (Dawn has used a black fabric for the backing)
170 cm x 220 cm (68 in x 86 in) of wadding

NOTIONS

Large sheet of strong cardboard or template plastic
Large sheet of paper
Plastic bags
Fineline permanent marker pen
Sandpaper board
Pencil, B
Pencil for marking black fabric, silver or yellow
Chalk dispenser or washable marker pencil

Sewing thread, black
Fabric scissors
Paper scissors
Glass-headed pins
Betweens needles, size 9 or 10, for piecing and quilting
Long thin needle for basting or safety pins (approximately 450)
Quilting hoop or frame

MAKING TEMPLATES

See the templates and the quilting pattern on the Pull Out Pattern Sheet. Using the marker pen, trace templates A to P onto the template plastic or photocopy the diagram of the full house block on the pattern sheet and paste it onto the cardboard, then cut out the required templates A to O. You could draw the house diagram on graph paper to ensure no distortion takes place during photocopying. The sections of the house not marked by a letter are duplicate shapes.

CUTTING

STEP ONE

Cut the borders and sashing strips down the length of the black fabric. A seam allowance of 6 mm ($\frac{1}{4}$ in) is included in all measurements for borders and sashing strips as well as an additional allowance of 4 cm (1$\frac{1}{2}$ in)

added to the length to allow for discrepancies. Always check the size of your own quilt before cutting the borders. Cut two 26.2 cm x 150 cm (10$\frac{1}{2}$ in x 60$\frac{1}{2}$ in) short borders, two 31.2 cm x 162 cm (12$\frac{1}{2}$ x 65 in) long borders, three 10.2 cm x 112 cm (4 in x 44 in) long sashing pieces, eight 10.2 cm x 31.2 cm (4 in x 12$\frac{1}{2}$ in) short sashing strips. Cut two 9 cm x 210 cm (3$\frac{1}{2}$ in x 84 in) and two 9 cm x 162 cm (3$\frac{1}{2}$ in x 65 in) lengths for the binding.

STEP TWO

Cut the following pieces from the black fabric: twenty-four A, twelve C, twelve D, twelve Dr, twelve F (reverse the template when marking the back of the fabric), twelve H, twenty-four M, twelve N and twelve O.

The Schoolhouse block

STEP THREE

From each of the twelve brightly coloured fabrics, cut two B, one E (reverse the template when marking the back of the fabric), one G, one I, two J, two K, one L and two P.

STEP FOUR

Assemble the pieces for each block and store them in separate plastic bags.

PIECING

STEP ONE

Following the block diagram, pin the pieces required for each block onto a large sheet of paper. Assemble the house block, using the piecing diagram in figure 1.

STEP TWO

Sew three house blocks together in a row, using two short sashing strips to separate them. Make four rows.

STEP THREE

Sew the four rows together alternating them with three long sashing strips.

FOR THE BORDERS

Attach the short borders to the sides of the pieced top, then attach the long borders to the top and bottom.

ASSEMBLING

STEP ONE

Using the marker pen, trace the tree quilting pattern onto the template plastic and cut it out. Using the photograph as a guide, mark the quilt top with trees using the chalk dispenser or a pencil. Do not use an ordinary colouring pencil to mark your quilt.

STEP TWO

Place the backing fabric face down on the floor or a table. Secure it with pins or tape. Centre the wadding, then the quilt top, face upwards on top. Smooth each layer as it is put down. Secure the three layers together with safety pins at 10 cm (4 in) intervals or baste the layers together.

QUILTING

Using the quilting thread, hoop and quilting needle, hand-quilt the entire quilt. For further information on hand-quilting see page 78.

FINISHING

STEP ONE

Carefully trim the wadding and the backing to the size of the quilt top.

STEP TWO

Press the black binding strips over double. Stitch the binding to the right side of the quilt with the raw edges matching. Stitch the sides first. Turn the folded edge of the binding to the back of the quilt.

STEP THREE

Stitch the top and bottom, allowing at least 12 mm ($\frac{1}{2}$ in) to extend beyond the quilt on both ends. Turn the folded edge of this binding to the back of the quilt. Slipstitch all the binding into place. At each corner, tuck in the excess binding to cover the raw edge.

Don't forget to sign and date your quilt.

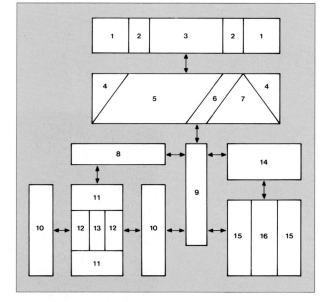

Fig. 1: Piecing the Schoolhouse block

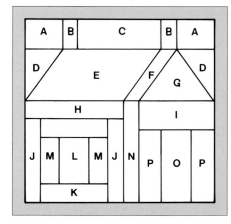

Block diagram

51

A FINE ROMANCE

By Ros Stinson

I really enjoy the effect of fine hand-quilting on plain fabric and invariably choose a design that incorporates this feature. The quilt 'Romance' which appeared in *Quiltmaker* Spring/Summer '88 provided wonderful spaces for quilting and, with the addition of an appliquéd swag (my other love), I had the basis for my quilt.
[We are grateful to *Quiltmaker* for permission to publish this quilt design.]

FINISHED SIZE

Quilt: 300 cm (118 in) square
Block size: 28 cm (11 in) square
Total number of blocks: twenty-four

Hand-pieced and hand-quilted

FABRIC QUANTITIES

7 m (7³/₄ yd) of cream fabric
80 cm (32 in) of mushroom-coloured fabric
3 m (3¹/₃ yd) of terracotta-coloured fabric
1.6 m (1³/₄ yd) of sage green checked fabric
5.5 m (6 yd) of dark green fabric
1.5 m (1²/₃ yd) of floral fabric

9.3 m (10¹/₃ yd) of cream homespun for the backing
310 cm (124 in) square of wadding

NOTIONS

Template plastic
Fineline permanent marker pen
Sandpaper board
Pencil, B
28 cm (11 in) square of thick cardboard for a template, or a rotary cutter, cutting board and large square ruler
Thin cardboard for the appliqué
38 cm (15 in) square of architect's tracing paper
Medium felt-tip pen
Matching sewing thread (mid- and dark green, cream and terracotta for the appliqué)

Quilting thread, cream
Fabric scissors
Paper scissors
Glass-headed pins
Betweens needles, size 9 or 10, for piecing and quilting
Long thin needle for basting
Quilting hoop
Plastic bags
Large sheet of paper

MAKING TEMPLATES

See the templates and the quilting patterns on the Pull Out Pattern Sheet. Note that the templates do not include seam allowances.

Using the marker pen, trace the templates C, D, E and F onto the template plastic. Trace C and E again and reverse the cut-out shapes, before

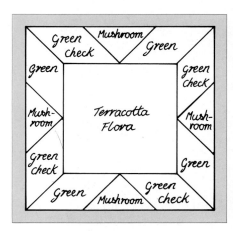

Block diagram

The pieced block

Quilting the cream square

marking them Cr and Er respectively. Trace a complete B by completing one half as shown and then the other adjoining half or draft a complete square of 16 cm (6¹/₄ in). Trace the templates G to N for the appliqué onto the template plastic. Cut inside the line when cutting them out. Mark each template with the grain line, then cut the templates out carefully.

CUTTING

All the cutting instructions are given below. You may wish to cut everything out at once or cut out each block as required. Make sure that if borders or bindings are required, that these are cut out first. All seam allowances are included in the border measurements. To mark the fabric, place the templates on the wrong side of the fabric and draw around them with the pencil. This pencil line will be your sewing line. Take care to leave space between each shape to allow for seams. Cut out each piece approximately 6 mm (¹/₄ in) from the sewing line.

Cut out the following pieces and store them in separate plastic bags for easy identification:

From the cream fabric, first cut four 29.2 cm x 310 cm (11¹/₂ in x 124 in) pieces down the length for the border; then, cut twenty-five A, using the card-board square or the rotary cutter and square ruler; then, cut one hundred and twelve D.

From the mushroom-coloured fabric, cut ninety-six D.

From the terracotta-coloured fabric, cut one hundred and twelve E, one hundred and twelve Er and twenty-eight J.

From the green checked fabric, cut ninety-six Cr, fourteen K, twenty-eight I, twenty-eight M, and twenty-eight N. From the dark green fabric, cut thirteen 9 cm (3¹/₂ in) wide strips across the width of the fabric for the binding; then, from the remaining fabric, cut ninety-six C, sixty-four F and twenty-eight G.

From the floral fabric, cut twenty-four B, fourteen H, fourteen L and fourteen M.

PIECING

STEP ONE

For each block you will need: one B in the floral fabric, four C in the dark green fabric, four Cr in the green checked fabric and four D in the mushroom-coloured fabric. Assemble the pieces for a block on the large sheet of paper, using the block diagram as your guide. Use a single pin to secure each piece in place.

STEP TWO

Attach a dark green C and green checked Cr to either side of a mushroom-coloured triangle D. Make four of these units, then sew one to each side of a central floral square. Complete the block by stitching the corners. Make twenty-four blocks.

STEP THREE

To complete a sashing unit, sew a terracotta E and Er to a cream triangle D (Fig. 1). Make one hundred and twelve sashing units.

STEP FOUR

Three different rows are required to complete the pieced quilt.
Row 1: Join eight dark green F squares alternating with seven sashing strips. Make eight rows.
Row 2: Join a sashing strip, an A block, a sashing strip, a pieced block, a sashing strip and so on until you have joined four A blocks and three pieced blocks. Make four rows.
Row 3: Join a sashing strip, a pieced block, a sashing strip, an A block, a sashing strip and so on, until you have joined four pieced blocks and three A blocks. Make three rows.

STEP FIVE

Using the photograph as a guide, join the rows together in the following sequence: row 1, row 2, row 1, row 3, row 1 and so on.

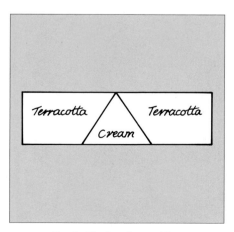

Fig. 1: Piecing the sashing

Fig. 2: The order of appliqué

FOR THE BORDERS

STEP ONE

Mark the position for the appliqué swags evenly along the cream border pieces with light pencil marks. Use the quilt photograph as a guide for the placement. Mark the position of the green swags first, then alternate motifs 1 and 2 between each swag.

STEP TWO

Following the instructions for appliqué on page 76 and the order indicated in figure 2, complete each border, except for the motifs on the corners.

STEP 3

Attach the appliquéd borders to the pieced top, mitring the corners. Complete the border appliqué by adding the final corner appliqués. Note that each of the motifs has been used twice.

The corner of the quilt, showing the appliqué and quilting pattern

ASSEMBLING

STEP ONE

Cut the backing fabric into three equal lengths, each 310 cm (124 in). Remove the selvages, then rejoin the pieces to form the backing, 310 cm x 330 cm (121 in x 138 in).

STEP TWO

Trace the quilting pattern from templates A and D onto the architect's tracing paper. You will need to rotate your paper to complete the four quarters of pattern A (Fig. 3). Go over the tracing, using the medium felt-tip pen.

STEP THREE

Position the complete quilting pattern under each cream square, centring it carefully. Trace the quilting pattern onto the quilt using the pencil. A light pencil line will be barely visible when you have finished quilting.

STEP FOUR

Draw the grid lines for quilting on the border using a ruler and pencil. The grid lines are drawn parallel to the mitred corner and from the feature points of each block. Use the close-up photograph to guide you.

STEP FIVE

Lay the backing fabric face down. Place the wadding and the quilt top (face upwards) on top. You will need a very large space to do this. A table tennis table is ideal. Smooth out each layer carefully. Baste the three layers together. Trim any unnecessary fabric from the backing, then roll over and baste the raw edges of the quilt to protect them during quilting.

QUILTING

Using the quilting thread, quilting needles and hoop, hand-quilt the entire quilt. The borders are easily quilted using a square quilting frame.

FINISHING

STEP ONE

Carefully trim the wadding and the backing to the size of the quilt top.

STEP TWO

Join the binding strips already cut to form four 304 cm (122 in) lengths. Fold the strips over double. Machine-stitch the strips to the right side of the quilt on two opposite sides, with the raw edges matching. Note that at least 12 mm (1/2 in) of excess binding extends beyond the edge of the quilt. Turn the folded edge of the binding to the back of the quilt.

STEP THREE

Sew the binding to the other two sides. Fold the excess in to cover the raw edges. Fold the binding over to the back of the quilt. Slipstitch all the binding in place.

Don't forget to sign and date your quilt.

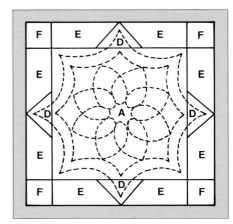

Fig. 3: The complete quilting pattern

WORLD WITHOUT END

By Lea Lane

Scrappy quilts represent the traditions of quiltmaking to me. With so little fabric available, any textile was treasured and incorporated into wonderful patterns by our enterprising ancestors. I like the idea of using small scraps which have little obvious value, and creating a beautiful quilt, just as so many have done before me.

FINISHED SIZE

Quilt: approximately 150 cm x 230 cm (60 in x 92 in)
Block size: 20 cm (8 in) square
Total number of blocks: sixty

Hand-pieced and hand-quilted

FABRIC QUANTITIES

3.2 m (3¹/₂ yd) of yellow fabric
Sixty large scraps of dark fabrics
Smaller scraps of sixty medium and sixty light fabrics
2.4 m (2²/₃ yd) of a large print fabric for the border
4.8 m (5¹/₃ yd) of fabric for the backing
235 cm x 155 cm (94 in x 61¹/₂ in) of wadding

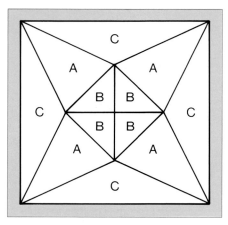

Block diagram

NOTIONS

Template plastic
Fineline permanent marker pen
Sandpaper board
Large sheet of paper
Pencil, B
Pencil for marking dark fabrics, silver or yellow
Matching sewing thread (mid-grey will blend with most fabrics)
Quilting thread, cream
Fabric scissors
Paper scissors
Glass-headed pins
Betweens needles, size 9 or 10, for piecing and quilting
Long thin needle for basting or 4 cm (1¹/₂ in) safety pins
6 mm (¹/₄ in) wide masking tape
Masking tape
Quilting hoop, approximately 45 cm (18 in)

MAKING TEMPLATES

See the templates on page 60. Note that the templates do not include seam allowances.

Using the marker pen, trace templates A, B, and C onto the template plastic. Mark the grain line on each one, then cut them out carefully.

CUTTING

STEP ONE

From the yellow fabric cut two pieces 6.2 cm x 220 cm (2¹/₂ in x 88 in) and one piece 6.2 cm x 280 cm (2¹/₂ in x 112 in) down the length of the fabric for the inner border. Seam allowances of 6 mm (¹/₄ in) are included and an additional 5 cm (2 in) is allowed on both ends for the mitre.

STEP TWO

For each block, cut the following pieces: four C from the yellow fabric, four A from the dark scraps, two B from the medium scraps, and two B from the light scraps. Use a large flat surface to mark out the yellow fabric. Carefully trace around two hundred and forty C triangles on the yellow fabric, leaving space between each one for seams. The cutting diagram in figure 1 will assist you with economic use of fabric. The pencil line will be your sewing line. Cut out each piece approximately 6 mm (¹/₄ in) from the sewing line.
HINT: You may wish to cut all the yellow triangles first and only cut out the dark, medium and light fabrics when you are ready to piece the next block. This will eliminate storage problems for all the pieces.

PIECING

STEP ONE

Assemble the pieces for one block on a large piece of paper using the block diagram as your guide. Use a single pin to secure each piece in place.

STEP TWO

Following the piecing diagram in figure 2, sew the central square first, using two medium and two light B pieces. Attach two A pieces on opposite sides of the central square, then sew two yellow C triangles on either side of the two remaining A. Finally, sew these units to the unit with the central square. Make sixty blocks.

STEP THREE

Sew the blocks together in ten rows of six blocks each.

FOR THE INNER BORDER

STEP ONE

Cut one 6.2 cm x 280 cm (2$^1/_2$ in x 112 in) yellow border strip in half to make two pieces 140 cm (56 in) long. Seam allowances of 6 mm ($^1/_4$ in) are included in these measurements as is an additional allowance of 5 cm (2 in) on either end of the strip for the mitres. Pin, then sew them to the top and bottom of the pieced top, matching centres and beginning and ending the stitching 6 mm ($^1/_4$ in) from the corners. Excess fabric will extend beyond the sides of the quilt top to allow for the mitred corners. Press the borders to the right side.

STEP TWO

Attach two 220 cm (88 in) long border strips to the sides of the quilt top in a similar manner. Mitre the corners of the border. See page 77 for tips on mitring.

FOR THE OUTER BORDER

Using the large print fabric, cut two 11.2 cm x 160 cm (4$^1/_2$ in x 64 in) and two 11.2 cm x 240 cm (4$^1/_2$ in x 96 in) strips for the outer border. Attach the outer border to the quilt top in the same way as the inner border, mitring the corners.

ASSEMBLING

STEP ONE

Cut the backing fabric into two 240 cm (96 in) lengths. Remove the selvages. Cut two 30 cm x 240 cm (12 in x 96 in) pieces from one of the lengths. Attach these two pieces on either side of the remaining 240 cm (96 in) length to make the complete backing, 170 cm x 240 cm (67 in x 96 in). Press.

STEP TWO

Since much of the quilting on this quilt is echo-quilting (follows the outline of the piecing), 6 mm ($^1/_4$ in) wide masking tape can be used to define the

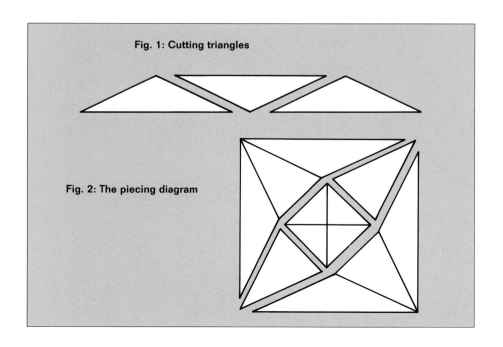

Fig. 1: Cutting triangles

Fig. 2: The piecing diagram

quilting line. See page 77 for tips on this use of masking tape. You can use the border quilting pattern photographed here or use one of your own. NOTE: The centre of each block is quilted differently. Make up your own designs as you come to each block.

STEP THREE

Lay the backing fabric face down and anchor it to the floor or table top using safety pins or masking tape. Centre the wadding on top, then the quilt top on top of that, face upwards. Smooth out each layer as it is put down. Secure the layers of the quilt sandwich with safety pins or basting.

STEP FOUR

Roll the raw edges of the quilt over onto the front and baste them in place to protect the edges during the quilting process.

QUILTING

Using the quilting thread, hoop and a quilting needle, hand-quilt the entire quilt. Begin your quilting in the centre of the quilt and work towards the edges. With most of the quilting completed, the rolled edges can be undone and the final border quilted without a hoop or a quilting frame.

FINISHING

STEP ONE

Carefully trim the wadding and the backing to the size of the quilt top.

STEP TWO

Cut 9 cm ($3^1/_2$ in) wide binding strips and join them to create a length equal to the perimeter of the quilt, approximately 7.8 m ($8^2/_3$ yd). Fold the strip over double as you attach it to the quilt, stitching it to the right side of the quilt, and matching the raw edges. Begin attaching the binding in the centre of one side and mitre the corners. Finish by overlapping the raw edge of the binding at the beginning with 12 mm ($^1/_2$ in) of binding at the end. Turn under the raw edges and stitch.

STEP THREE

Turn the binding over to the quilt back, covering the stitching lines and folding tucks diagonally at the corners. Slipstitch the binding into place.

Don't forget to sign and date your quilt.

The quilting pattern

A corner of the quilt showing the quilted border

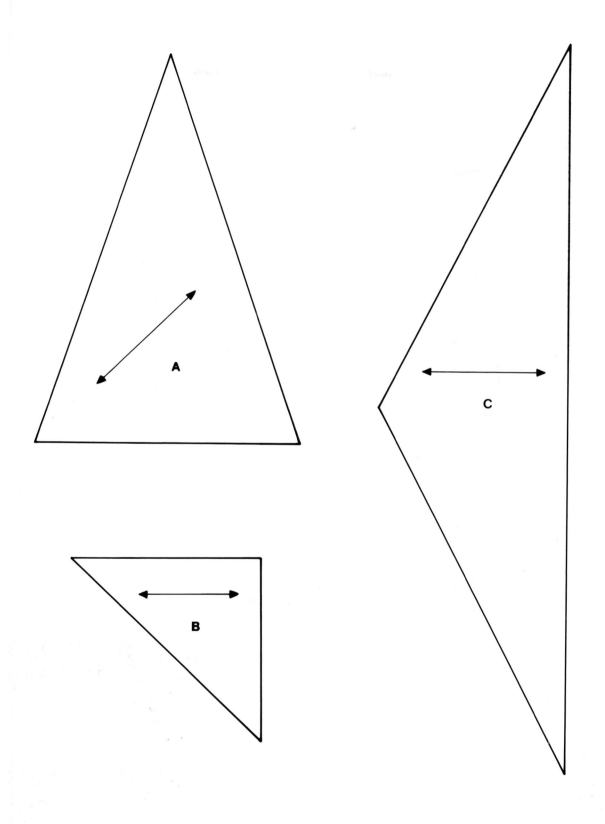

AUTUMN LEAVES FALLING

By Sally Bell

Autumn and the colours of the falling leaves inspired me to make this small fun quilt. Using black fabric for the background highlighted the other fabrics, which were mostly leftovers from other projects. The green leaves all point to the sky, while the red yellow, brown and ochre leaves fall randomly to scatter on the ground below.

FINISHED SIZE

Quilt: approximately 91.5 cm (34 in) square

Block size: 12 cm (4½ in – this is not an exact conversion but will work best if you are drafting your own block and using imperial measurements)

Total number of blocks: thirty-six

Hand-pieced and hand-quilted

FABRIC QUANTITIES

Thirty-six different scraps of autumn-toned fabrics

2.3 m (2½ yd) of black fabric for the blocks, sashing and borders

1 m (1½ yd) of fabric for the backing

1 m (1½ yd) square of wadding

NOTIONS

Template plastic
Craft knife
Fineline permanent marker pen
Sandpaper board
Pencil, B
Sheet of paper or large handkerchief
Pencil for marking dark fabrics, silver or yellow
Matching sewing thread
Quilting thread, black
Fabric scissors
Paper scissors
Glass-headed pins
Betweens needles, size 9 or 10, for piecing and quilting
Long thin needle for basting or safety pins (approximately 200)
Quilting hoop
Chalk dispenser or tailor's chalk

MAKING TEMPLATES

See the templates and the quilting pattern on page 66. Note that the templates do not include seam allowances.

Trace the templates A, B, C and D onto the template plastic. Trace a second C template and mark it Cr on the reverse side to give the mirror image of C. Mark the grain line on each template, then carefully cut out the templates.

CUTTING

STEP ONE

Place fabric wrong side up on the sandpaper board. With the grain lines matching, carefully trace around the required number of templates for each fabric, using the pencil. This pencil line will be your sewing line. Leave enough space between each shape to allow for seams. Cut out each piece approximately 6 mm (¼ in) from the sewing line. Cut one C, one Cr and two D from each of the thirty-six different autumn-toned fabrics.

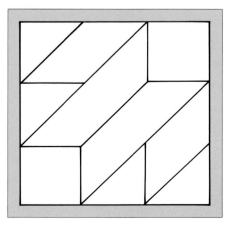

Block diagram

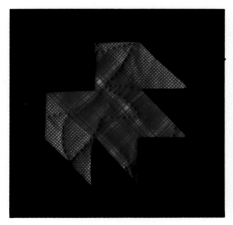

The pieced block

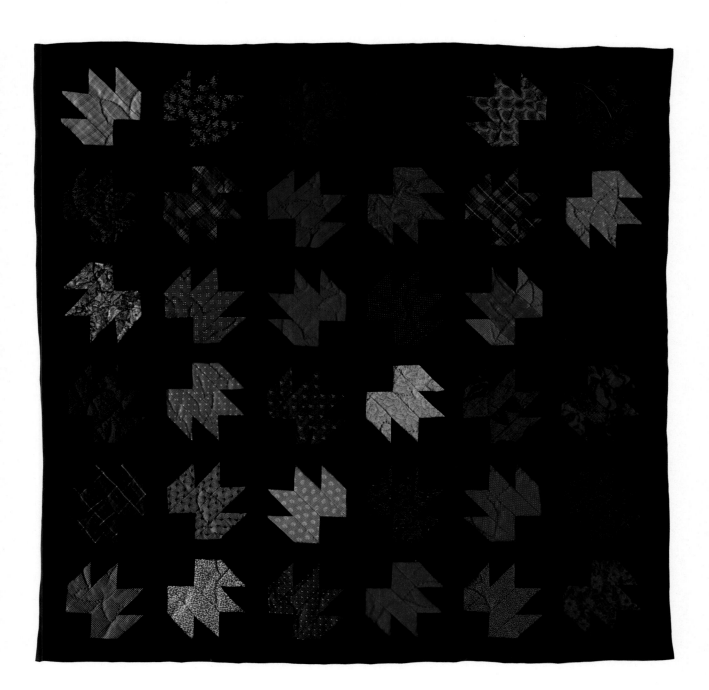

STEP TWO

Cut four strips, each 3.7 cm (1$\frac{1}{2}$ in) wide across the width of the black fabric. From these, cut off thirty 13.2 cm (5 in) lengths for the short sashing. Cut five 3.7 cm (1$\frac{1}{2}$ in) wide strips across the width of the fabric. Trim each of these to 88.5 cm (33 in) for the long sashing. From the remaining black fabric, cut one hundred and forty-four A and seventy-two B.

STEP THREE

Check the measurements of your quilt before cutting the borders. Cut four 4.7 cm (2 in) wide strips across the width of the fabric. Trim each of these to 95.5 cm (38 in) for the borders. Cut four 9 cm (3$\frac{1}{2}$ in) wide strips across the width of the fabric. Trim each of these to approximately 95 cm (38 in) for the binding. Seam allowances are included in these measurements.

PIECING

STEP ONE

Following the block diagram, pin the pieces required for each block onto the sheet of paper or the large handkerchief. Use only one pin in each piece to hold it in place.

STEP TWO

Following figure 1, assemble the leaf block as shown. Make thirty-six leaf blocks, using a different autumn-toned fabric in each one.
HINT: To keep the black triangles and squares used in each block together, thread your needle with a long thread, knotted at one end. Then thread each square onto the thread. Repeat the process for the triangles. When you need a piece, just slide it off the thread.

STEP THREE

Join six blocks in a row by sewing a short sashing piece in between the blocks. You will need six blocks and five short sashing pieces to complete each row. Make six rows.
NOTE: You can sew the sashings by hand or by machine. Machine-sewing tends to be stronger.

STEP FOUR

Join the six completed rows with the five long sashings in between to complete the quilt top.

FOR THE BORDER

Attach two black border strips to opposite sides of the quilt top. Trim. Attach the remaining two strips to the other two sides of the quilt top.

ASSEMBLING

STEP ONE

Trace the quilting pattern onto the template plastic, then cut it out using the craft knife. Using the pencil, mark the leaf pattern randomly over the quilt top. If it is difficult to see the pencil line, you could use a chalk dispenser or tailor's chalk. First test it on a small sample of the fabric to ensure that all marks can be removed after quilting. The pencil line will wear off fairly quickly.
HINT: You could pick an autumn leaf from your garden as Sally did and use it as the pattern for the quilting, or perhaps you could use several leaves to give a different effect.

STEP TWO

Place the backing face down on a table with the wadding on top and the quilt top on top of that, face upwards. Smooth out all the layers, then pin them together with safety pins at about 10 cm (4 in) intervals or baste.

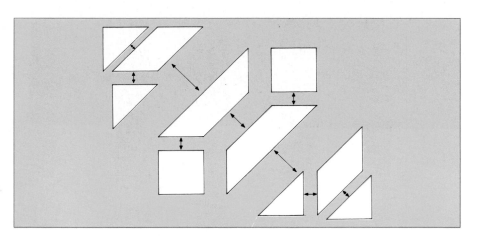

Fig. 1: The piecing diagram

QUILTING

Using black quilting thread, a size 9 or 10 betweens needle and the quilting hoop, hand-quilt the entire quilt. For tips on hand-quilting, see page 78.

FINISHING

STEP ONE

Carefully trim the wadding and the backing to the size of the quilt top.

STEP TWO

Press the black binding strips over double with the wrong sides together. Machine-stitch the binding to the right side of the quilt with the raw edges matching. Stitch the long sides first. Turn the folded edge of the binding to the back of the quilt.

STEP THREE

Attach the binding to the other two sides, allowing 12 mm ($\frac{1}{2}$ in) to extend beyond the quilt on both ends. Turn the folded edge of this binding to the back of the quilt. Slipstitch all the binding into place. At each corner, tuck in the excess binding to cover the raw edges.

Don't forget to sign and date your quilt.

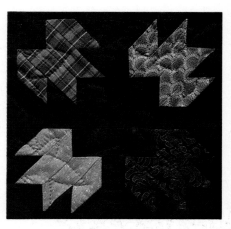

Four joined blocks

SCRAPPY TRIANGLES

By Evelyn Seymour

My collection of charm pieces was getting out of hand. I had cut a triangle
from each fabric I already had and had begged more fabric from friends,
but I had ended up with so many fabrics that I didn't know if I was doubling
up. To make it easier to keep track, I decided to join the triangles in
colour groupings. Fifty-four blocks later, I had my quilt.

FINISHED SIZE

Quilt: approximately 162 cm x 243 cm
  (63 in x 94^1/$_2$ in – this is not an exact
  conversion, but is the size based
  on using a 10^1/$_2$ in block)
Block size: 27 cm (10^1/$_2$ in)
Total number of blocks: fifty-four
  blocks set seven blocks across
  by nine blocks down

Hand-pieced and tied

FABRIC SUGGESTIONS

Each block in this quilt features one
colour. You will need scraps of eighteen different fabrics in the same colour
for each block. Choose colours that
feature most in your scrap bag, then
beg, borrow or steal the rest from
your friends. You will need light,
medium and dark colours to achieve
the colour-wash effect.

FABRIC QUANTITIES

Scraps of fabrics in the appropriate
  colours
5.2 m (5^3/$_4$ yd) of fabric for the
  backing of wadding
170 cm x 250 cm (67 in x 97 in) of
  medium-weight wadding
0.9 m (1 yd) of fabric for the binding

NOTIONS

Template plastic
Fineline permanent marker pen
Sandpaper board
Wide masking tape
Pencil, B
Sewing threads in light, medium and
  dark grey to blend with all the
  fabrics
Fabric scissors
Paper scissors
Thread for tying: knitting cotton,
  perle thread or thick crochet
  thread
Glass-headed pins
Betweens needles, size 9 or 10, for
  the piecing
Safety pins, at least 400

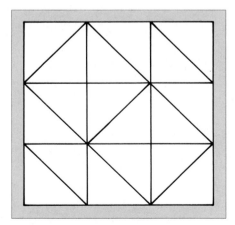

Block diagram

TEMPLATES

See the template on page 70. Note that
the template does not include seam
allowances. Trace around the template
onto the template plastic, using the
marker pen. Mark the grain line
on the template. Cut out the template
carefully.

CUTTING

STEP ONE

Select eighteen scraps of the same-
coloured fabric, but with a variety of
print sizes and colour tones. Refer to
the photographs for a guide.

STEP TWO

Place the fabric with the wrong side up
on the sandpaper board. Place the
template on the fabric, matching the
grain lines. Trace carefully around the
template with the pencil. This pencil
line will be your sewing line. Continue,
marking templates in this way, leaving
space between each one to allow for
the seams. Cut around each piece
6 mm (^{1}/$_4$ in) from the pencil line.

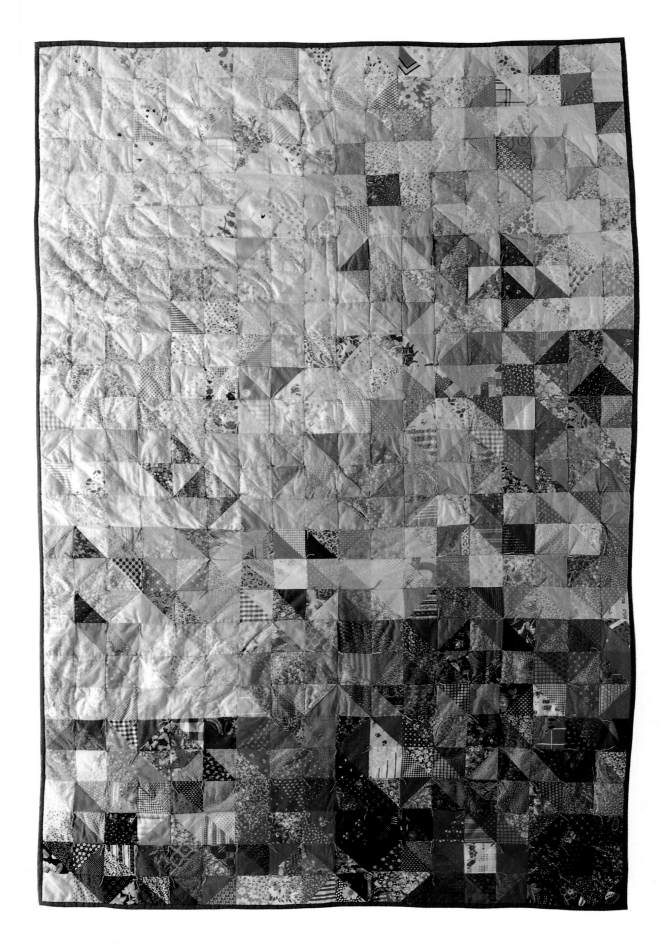

PIECING

Assemble sixteen triangles on a large piece of paper as indicated in the block diagram. Pin them in place using one pin for each triangle. Do not be too particular about which shades of your chosen colour you use. The random nature of your selection will add to the charm of the quilt.

STEP TWO

Sew pairs of triangles together to make nine small squares. Sew three square units together to make a row. Sew these rows together to complete the block.

STEP THREE

Make fifty-three more blocks in the same way, using dark, medium and light colours to achieve the colour-wash effect.

STEP FOUR

Press all the blocks carefully. Spread them out on a table or on the floor to check that you are happy with the colour and effect, then join them in nine rows of seven blocks. Join the rows to complete the quilt top.

The pieced block

ASSEMBLING

STEP ONE

Cut the backing fabric into two pieces, each 2.6 m ($2^7/_8$ yd) long. Remove the selvages, then join them lengthwise to form the backing, 2.2 m x 2.6 m ($2^1/_4$ yd x $2^7/_8$ yd). As the quilt top is only 162 cm x 243 cm (63 in x $94^1/_2$ in), you can trim the width a little, if you wish.

STEP TWO

Place the backing face down on the floor or a very large table. Smooth out any wrinkles and anchor the backing to the floor with large safety pins (in the case of carpet) or tape it down. Place the wadding on top, then the quilt top face upwards on the top of the wadding. Pin-baste the three layers together, using a safety pin at each spot to be tied.

TYING

Thread the needle with the thread of your choice. Do not knot the end. Work two backstitches over the first pin, leaving enough thread at the beginning to be tied. Without cutting the thread, move on to the next pin, leaving the thread slack between the pins. Make two backstitches over the next pin and so on. Continue until there is insufficient thread to reach the next pin. Cut the threads between the pins and tie the ends in a square knot. Trim the ends.
HINT: A tied or tufted quilt can be finished very quickly and allows you the luxury of very thick wadding. You can tie with knots at the front or the back, create fluffy tufts, make bows, or use buttons.

FINISHING

STEP ONE

Carefully trim the wadding and the backing to the size of the quilt top.

STEP TWO

Cut ten 9 cm ($3^1/_2$ in) wide strips across the width of the binding fabric. Join the strips to make two pieces 247 cm ($97^1/_2$ in) long and two pieces 166 cm ($65^1/_2$ in) long. Fold the strips over double with the wrong sides facing. Machine-stitch the binding to the right side of the quilt with the raw edges even. Stitch the long sides first. Turn the folded edge of the binding to the back of the quilt.

STEP THREE

Attach the binding to the other two sides, allowing at least 12 mm ($^1/_2$ in) to extend beyond the quilt on both ends. Turn the folded edge of this binding to the back of the quilt. Slipstitch all the binding in place, folding in the excess length at the ends to cover the raw edges.

Don't forget to sign and date your quilt.

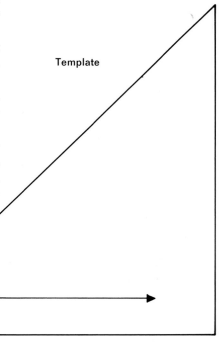

Template

YOU WILL NEED

Although you probably have much of the equipment used in quiltmaking if you are a sewer, it is important to collect all the equipment you will need for a project and store it in one place. You may even like to decorate a basket especially for this purpose and keep it just for quilting supplies. If any equipment needs to be purchased, buy the best you can afford, and keep everything in good condition.

FABRIC

Although it is often thought that quilts are made with scraps, many scraps collected from dressmaking and other household sewing are not appropriate for making quilts. They have different fibre content, weave, weight and scale of design – all important considerations for the quiltmaker.

Because of this, many quiltmakers prefer to buy fabrics with a weave that is not too tight (such as sheeting), or too loose (such as flannelette), of medium weight, not heavy (such as wool) or light (such as organza), and all cotton.

The one hundred per cent cotton fabrics stitch more smoothly, crease better for appliqué and finger-pressing, and unravel less. A more experienced quilter may choose to use a more difficult fabric to work with for a particular effect, but the beginner is advised to use one hundred per cent cotton fabrics. In fact, many quilters, regardless of experience, work only with cottons. The quilts in this book are all made from 110 cm (45 in) wide one hundred per cent cotton which, for the most part, have been designed to be used especially for patchwork and quilting, and are available from specialist quilting supply shops.

COLOUR

The colours chosen by the artist for any particular quilt may not be to your liking. Experiment with different combinations of colour and print to achieve a more personal look.

Probably the most intimidating element in quilt design is the choice of colour, but it is also the most exciting. To help with your initial selection of colours, choose a fabric you really like. Use the colours in the fabric to help with your selection of other fabrics. Introduce an element of surprise by including a complementary colour outside your chosen range, and add a further dimension to your palette by embracing some colours just beyond your colour range; for example in a blue and white quilt include aqua and mauve.

With the wide selection of fabrics available don't hesitate to experiment with unexpected colours and patterns to brighten and individualise your quilt.

PATTERN

Keep scale in mind when combining prints. For a more appealing quilt, include small, medium and large prints in your palette. Small-scale prints will appear solid when looked at from a distance and can be used effectively to replace a solid-coloured fabric. Large-scale prints will add a lot of interest and provide good contrast with small and medium prints. The value, or how light or dark a fabric is, is crucial to the overall effect of the quilt. Placement of light, medium or dark fabrics can change a design completely. Use a range of values in your quilt for a successful result. Most quilts are enhanced by the inclusion of a very dark fabric. Fabrics that contrast both in scale and value work well placed next to each other. Geometric prints add variety and an element of surprise to any design.

CHOOSING FABRIC

While the techniques used in sewing patchwork and quilting are easily learned, the art of choosing a stunning colour scheme and interesting fabrics is only learned with experience. Think of your fabric as an artist's palette. Discard fabric that isn't working in your design, just as an artist would wash his brush. Get a better idea of what appeals to you by studying both old and new quilts and see how the artist has achieved a particular effect. At the same time, be content with what appeals to you, and don't allow the choice of fabric to be such an agony that it stops you enjoying the choosing. Part of the joy of patchwork and quilting is the creativity inspired by the selection and purchase of fabric. The more you make quilts, the more fabric you will accumulate. Purchase only the best quality fabrics. The results will be much more pleasing and the quilt will last much longer.

Separate fabrics into groups by colour and store them folded on shelves or in boxes. A shoe box is an ideal way to store smaller pieces of fabric of the same colour.

Scissors, templates, coloured cottons and patterned fabrics are just some of the equipment you will need to make your quilt

PREPARATION

Wash your fabrics before you use them to remove any excess dye and sizing. Most fabrics can be washed together in the washing machine, but you may wish to wash light and dark fabrics separately, just to be sure. If you have any concerns about a particular fabric, and are afraid that it might 'bleed', soak a scrap in warm water for one hour. If the dye runs, soak the whole piece in a solution of three parts water to one part vinegar. If dye is still running after this treatment, discard the fabric.

Fabrics may be dried in a tumble dryer. Remove them while they are still just damp to avoid too many creases, then press them.

WADDING

Wadding (or batting or batt, as it is also called) is the padding between the quilt top and the backing fabric. Traditionally, cotton batts were used, requiring many hours of quilting to provide stability. These days, most quilters prefer to use the readily available polyester wadding which comes in a variety of thicknesses. Remember, the thinner the wadding, the smaller the quilting stitch it is possible to do. Cotton wadding is now available in a more stable form and is chosen by quilters who wish to give a new quilt an antique feel and appearance.

Wool and polyester/wool wadding is also available and makes a delightfully soft quilt. Dark wadding, made from dark fleece is also available.

FOR SEWING

NEEDLES

Use quilting (betweens) needles for all piecing, appliqué and quilting. Most quilters use size 9 or 10 needles, but you can purchase a packet of mixed needles to determine which suits you best. Experienced quilters prefer size 12 betweens to achieve the perfect tiny quilting stitch.

You may prefer to keep your betweens needles just for quilting and use a size 7 or 8 embroidery (crewel) needle for piecing and appliqué. These are longer and have a larger eye for ease of threading. Experiment until you find the needles you are most comfortable using.

For basting, use a long thin needle which allows you to take many stitches at a time.

THIMBLE

A thimble should be worn on the middle finger of your sewing hand. If you are not used to wearing a thimble, initially it will feel awkward. Persevere, as it is only a matter of becoming accustomed to the thimble, and eventually you will not be able to do any sewing without it. A thimble is indispensable for pushing the needle through layers of fabric, especially when quilting.

Some quilters also like to wear a thimble, often leather, on the hand below the quilt. A variety of thimbles are available for you to try. Experiment until you find the one that suits you.

THREAD

Number 50 cotton thread is recommended for all hand-piecing and appliqué. Many fabric stores stock a wide range of polyester threads. These are not recommended as they are stronger than the fabric they would be sewing and could eventually cut the quilt. If cotton thread is unavailable, then choose cotton-covered polyester thread.

For the actual quilting, use cotton quilting thread. It has a special coating and is very strong. Quilting thread now comes in a delightful range of colours. If no satisfactory colour can be found, then coating a number 50 cotton thread with beeswax will do as a substitute.

Always thread your needle with thread as it comes off the spool. This way you will be sewing with the natural twist of the thread and avoiding knotting.

When sewing by hand, work with thread lengths of 45 cm (18 in) or less.

PINS

Glass-headed pins are recommended because they are very sharp and are easily manouevred through layers of fabric. They are also easily located if dropped or inadvertently left in a project. Discard any thick or rusted pins.

For pin-basting, use 4 cm (1¹/₂ in) safety pins. These are small enough to not mark the fabric, but large enough to go through the three layers of quilt top, wadding and backing.

QUILTING HOOPS AND FRAMES

To maintain an even tension during quilting, a hoop or frame is a must. The hoop is composed of two wooden rings, tightened by twisting a screw once the quilt is between the rings. Round hoops are available from 35 to 58 cm (14 to 23 in). Select the size you feel most comfortable with. An oval hoop is not recommended as it gives an uneven tension. See page 78 for the best way to use a hoop.

Hand-held square frames are also available and make the completion of the border much easier. Full-size quilting frames are handy for large projects or group efforts.

FOR MARKING AND CUTTING

SCISSORS

Good equipment is essential for all aspects of quilting but it is absolutely imperative that you have a good pair of sharp fabric scissors. They should be able to cut accurately and easily through several layers of fabric.

Paper scissors are needed for cutting paper, cardboard and template plastic. These materials will dull fabric scissors.

You may also wish to have on hand some embroidery scissors for cutting threads and some small scissors with very sharp points for clipping appliqué and cutting out small details.

ROTARY CUTTER AND MAT

While most of the projects in the book do not employ a rotary cutter for preparing the patchwork pieces, it is an excellent tool for cutting strips, straightening edges and cutting out large blocks. If you wish to use your machine to piece these designs, the rotary cutter becomes an essential tool for cutting multiple layers of fabric. Always use a self-healing mat when cutting with a rotary cutter and keep the shield over the blade when it is not in use. Replace any rusty blades.

RULERS

Include in your collection of equipment a variety of rulers for measuring, along with a double-sided tape measure showing both imperial and metric measurements.

You will need a regular 30 cm or 40 cm (12 in or 16 in) ruler for simple measuring, and a long transparent ruler suitable for use with the rotary cutter. These rulers are now available marked either with metric or imperial divisions and also have angled lines for ease of measurement and cutting. A small gridded ruler can be helpful in drawing accurate templates and marking seam allowances. A metre-long metal ruler is invaluable for marking grid lines across a quilt.

PENCILS

A variety of marking pencils is available on the market today, seeking to replace the traditional pencil as the tool for marking seam lines and quilting designs.

The water-soluble pen, while saving time in marking, can often cause problems later, with the washed-out colour reappearing. Follow the manufacturer's instructions carefully and be sure to test all markers on the fabrics you are using.

A soft B pencil, used lightly, will accomplish most marking needs, with the addition of a silver pencil and a chalk dispenser for marking dark fabrics. Keep all your pencils sharpened for accurate marking.

FOR TEMPLATE MAKING

TEMPLATE PLASTIC

Clear, gridded or almost-clear (frosted-on-one-side) sheets of plastic are excellent for making reusable templates, thus avoiding the ragged edges and corners typical of cardboard templates after several uses. You can draw on the plastic with a fineline permanent marker pen or, if you have the frosted plastic, with a pencil.

CRAFT OR UTILITY KNIFE

Available from art supply stores, these are essential when cutting stencils for quilting, or very thick cardboard. Change the blades frequently to ensure the best finish.

PAPER

Keep both squared and isometric grid paper on hand for accurate template making. Large sheets of gridded paper are available from most newsagents as well as A4 size. Graph paper is essential if you are keen to draft your own templates or if you plan to change the size of given ones.

Architect's tracing paper provides an attractive and more substantial alternative to the tracing paper found in most kitchens.

PROTRACTOR AND COMPASS

These are necessary additions to your equipment for drafting templates with unusual angles and geometric shapes, such as the hexagon, as well as curved and circular templates.

GLUE STICK

Keep one on hand for gluing graph paper to cardboard.

Choosing the correct fabric is crucial and with so many different patterns available the combinations are endless

YOU NEED TO KNOW

The quilts in this book are made mostly by hand, employing methods used before the discovery of the sewing machine, and still favoured by many quiltmakers today. Although slower then a machine-sewing, handwork enables the quilter to continue stitching while interacting with family and friends.

FOR PERFECT PATCHWORK

ROTARY CUTTING

Borders, sashing and binding strips should be cut first, before templates are used to mark the fabric. This can most easily be done using a rotary cutter and a self-healing cutting mat. All the measurements for borders and bindings are given with seam allowances included. Each set of instructions gives suggestions on whether these strips are best cut down the fabric or across it.

To use a rotary cutter, follow these steps:

1 Fold the fabric over double on the cutting mat, with selvages matching. Make sure the fold is smooth and flat. Fold the fabric over double again. Place a small square ruler or a large right-angled triangle on the fold and a long ruler on the left edge of the square ruler or triangle, just covering the raw edge of the fabric (reverse if left-handed Fig. 1).

2 Remove the small square ruler and holding the long ruler firmly in place, cut along the right-hand edge of the ruler with the rotary cutter, keeping the blade perpendicular and pushing it away from you.

3 Position the ruler on the edge of the fabric at the desired width, and cut (Fig. 2).

4 To cut sashing strips, cut a strip the required width of the strip and trim the selvages, then cut the required length.

TEMPLATES

The making of accurate templates is one of the most important aspects of pieced work.

The templates given in this book do NOT have a seam allowance included in the shape. Templates are used to mark the sewing line on the fabric, not the cutting line. Trace the templates onto template plastic, using a ruler and pen to mark straight sides and marking the corners with a dot first, then joining the dots to ensure accuracy.

Always mark fabric on the wrong side for piecing, using a pencil (B, yellow or silver) or a white chalk marker on dark fabric. For appliqué, mark templates on the right side of the fabric. Keep your pencils very sharp to ensure the lines are accurate.

Position the templates on the fabric at least 12 mm (1/2 in) apart so that seam allowances can be added when cutting (Fig. 3).

It is a good idea to use a sandpaper board when marking to prevent the fabric slipping.

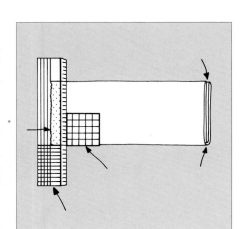

Fig. 1

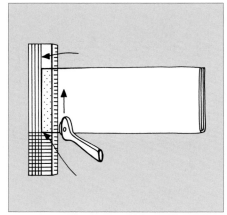

Fig. 2

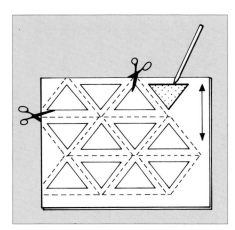

Fig. 3

HAND-PIECING

Pin shapes together with the right sides facing, placing pins at each corner and along the sewing lines (Fig. 4).

Thread the needle of your choice, knot the end of the thread and bring the needle up through the fabric exactly at the corner of the marked line. Beginning with a backstitch, sew along the sewing line, using a small running stitch (about eight stitches every 2.5 cm (1 in). Check the back occasionally to make sure you are still on the line. Finish at the other corner on the marked line, working several backstitches to secure the sewing.

For joining rows, match the seam lines on the two rows, with the right sides together. Insert pins exactly at the corners of each piece and as close as possible to each seam. As you sew to each seam, backstitch on one side of the seam, pass the needle through the seam, then backstitch again on the other side (Fig. 5).

HAND-APPLIQUE

There are two methods described here for hand-appliqué. Choose the one which best suits you. Or use both methods together, pre-basting difficult shapes and needle-turning for others.

For each method, clip any curved edges of the shape almost to the marked outline, allowing for ease of turning.

Pre-basting

This method gives a crisp outline and a high degree of accuracy. Cut out a cardboard shape for each piece being appliquéd. Place the fabric shape on the cardboard shape, turning the raw edges onto the back of the cardboard. Baste the fabric to the cardboard (Fig. 6). Press the piece carefully with a little spray starch for a very crisp finish. Remove the basting and the cardboard. Your shape is now ready to appliqué.

Finger or needle-turn method

This method is quicker, but without the degree of accuracy for the inexperienced quiltmaker. However, with practice, many quiltmakers achieve excellent results and it becomes their preferred method.

Pin the appliqué piece into position on the right side of the base fabric. Use your fingers and thumb to roll the seam allowance under, just hiding the marked sewing line. If your fingers obstruct the view, use your needle to tuck the seam allowance under. Trim the seam allowance to under 6 mm ($^1/_4$ in) for ease of turning (Fig. 7).

For both methods, use a thread to match the appliqué. Sew the appliqué piece to the base fabric using slipstitches that are very close

together, just catching a few threads of the fabric. A running stitch or blanket stitch can also be used.

BORDERS

Borders are used to frame a pieced top, or to increase its size. Choose fabrics for the border that reflect the 'feel' of the quilt. You may want to introduce a new fabric to complement what has already been completed or use a fabric in the pieced top. To select your border fabric, lay the fabric around the edge of the quilt top to see if it 'works'.

A narrow border inside the final border is often used to provide that extra sparkle (see 'Miniature Amish Baskets' on page 44).

Borders may have squared or mitred corners.

The instructions in this book give suggested measurements for borders, but it is always best to measure your own pieced top to be sure. Measure the finished pieced top across the middle both vertically and horizontally to give the quilt size.

Borders with square corners

For length, cut border strips the length of the quilt plus seam allowances. For width, cut border strips the width of the quilt plus twice the width of the border strip plus a seam allowance of 6 mm ($^1/_4$ in). The measurements for borders in this book all include seam

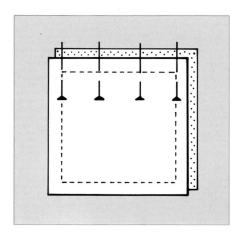

Fig. 4

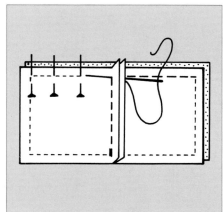

Fig. 5

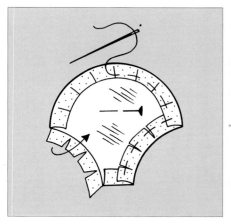

Fig. 6

allowances and an additional 4 cm (1½ in) in length. Trim them if necessary. Sew the border strips to the sides of the quilt top, then to the top and bottom (Fig. 8). Press the seams towards the darker fabric.

Borders with mitred corners

For length or width, cut the border strips the length or width of the quilt top plus twice the width of the border strip plus an extra 10 cm (4 in) for the mitring. Find the centre of each strip and the centre of the edge of the quilt by folding. Sew the border strips to two sides of the quilt top with the right sides together, matching centres. Begin and end the stitching 6 mm (¼ in) from the corners of the pieced top. The excess border fabric will extend beyond the edge of the quilt top, equally at both ends.

Sew the remaining border strips to the other two sides of the quilt in the same manner, making sure that the seam stops at the same place as the previous seam. Press.

On the wrong side, fold the border strips back at a forty-five degree angle so that they touch one another (Fig. 9). Matching creases and stitching exactly on the creases, beginning from the outside, stitch the mitres. Trim the excess seam allowance.

PREPARATION FOR QUILTING

Marking the quilting pattern

Secure and cut off all threads and trim the raw edges on the quilt top. Press the top thoroughly because you will not be able to press it again.

To mark the quilting pattern, place the stencil on the right side of the quilt top and trace around it with a pencil. These pencil lines will wear off very quickly. On dark fabrics, use a chalk dispenser. When marking calico or another light-coloured fabric, the design can be traced. Draw the quilting design onto paper, and draw over it with a black felt-tip pen. Place the pattern under the fabric, then trace it using a B pencil and pressing very lightly. A light under a glass-topped table will facilitate the tracing.

Straight quilting lines can be indicated with 6 mm (¼ in) wide masking tape after the quilt is pieced. Work only a small area at a time and remove the tape at the end of a working session to avoid sticky residue.

THE BACKING

Cut the backing at least 10 cm (4 in) larger all around than the quilt top. You may need to sew two or three lengths of fabric together to make the backing reach the required size. Trim the selvages before sewing and press the seams open to assist in quilting.

THE WADDING (BATTING)

Cut the wadding slightly smaller than the backing and a little larger than the quilt top. If your piece of wadding is not big enough then it may be pieced. Do not overlap pieces of wadding when joining them, just butt pieces together.

THE QUILT SANDWICH

Place the backing face down on the floor or on a large table, such as a table tennis table. Use masking tape or large safety pins (in the case of carpet) to secure the backing. Make sure the fabric is as smooth as it can be, and the corners are square. Centre the wadding on the backing and smooth it out. Next comes the quilt top, face up in the centre, with its edges parallel to the backing edges. Smooth the quilt top gently to remove any wrinkles (Fig. 10).

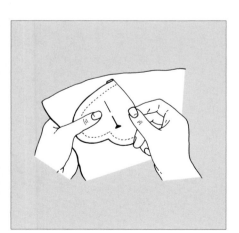

Fig. 7

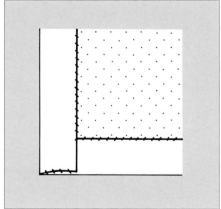

Fig. 8

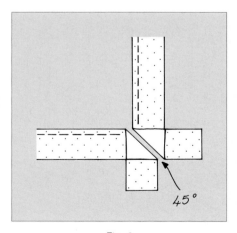

Fig. 9

BASTING

Thread your basting needle with a long thread of light-coloured cotton. Beginning at the centre, baste a diagonal line to each corner. Then complete a grid of horizontal and vertical lines, finishing with a row of basting around the edges (Fig. 11). Complete the basting by rolling the backing to the front, over the raw edges, and basting them in place to protect the raw edges during the quilting process. The more basting you do, the more secure will be the three layers. Alternatively the quilt may be pin-basted with safety pins. You will need about five hundred pins to baste a double-bed quilt. Place a safety pin approximately every 10 cm (4 in).

QUILTING

A hoop is essential to maintain consistent tension throughout the quilting process. The quilt layers will be held in place enabling you to work more quickly and evenly.

Place the inner circle of the hoop on a flat surface with the section of the quilt sandwich to be quilted over it. Loosen the screw on the outer loop, then put the outer hoop over the quilt and tighten the screw. If you have pin-basted, be careful to move any pins that might be caught in the hoop. The hoop defines the work area.

For borders, use a square frame or attach plain fabric to the edges of the quilt so that the hoop can hold the edges taut.

For quilting, one hand is under the quilt, the sewing hand on the top (Fig. 12).

HAND-QUILTING

Using a short between needle and quilting thread, thread the needle with a short length (approximately 45 cm (18 in)) of thread and knot the end.

Insert the needle through the quilt top and wadding, about 2.5 cm (1 in) from where you wish to start quilting. Bring the needle up at the point where you will begin and, with a quick pull, secure the knot under the quilt top, buried in the wadding. Now you are ready to begin quilting.

The hand-quilting stitch is a running stitch through the three layers of the quilt. While small stitches are highly prized, they are only achievable with practice. More importantly, keep the stitch size even with even spaces between them.

Begin to take short running stitches through all three layers towards your thumb, rocking the needle up and down on the thimble. The other hand is underneath the quilt to feel the needle tip and guide its return (Fig. 13). Take three or four stitches at a time and pull the thread firmly to give that lovely sculptured look.

To complete a line of quilting, make a small knot near the last stitch, backstitch and then run the thread through the wadding. Pull the thread through again, leaving the knot in the wadding.

MACHINE QUILTING

Pin-baste the quilt sandwich with 4cm (1½ in) safety pins at approximately 10 cm intervals. Begin quilting in the centre of the quilt, rolling the excess quilt for convenience in manoeuvring the quilt under the head of the sewing machine. There is no need to mark the quilt top if you are quilting in-the-ditch. For straight line, quilting a walking foot is extremely useful in feeding the three layers through the machine without puckering.

Make sure you machine-quilt in the same direction across the quilt to minimise shifting of the layers.

Free-form designs can be quilted using the sewing machine. Drop the feed dogs and attach a darning foot. Do not turn the fabric to follow the design but guide the quilt with your hands, imitating the tension created by a hoop.

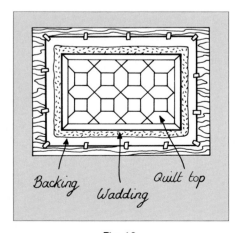

Fig. 10

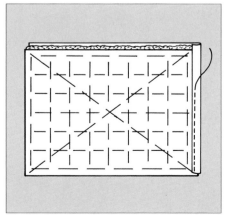

Fig. 11

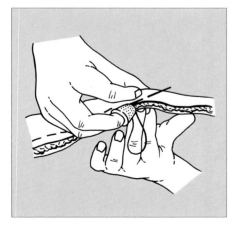

Fig. 12

BINDING.

For most quilts, 9 cm (3$\frac{1}{2}$ in) wide binding is used, folded over double, lengthwise. Use a narrower binding for miniature quilts. Before attaching the binding, trim the wadding and the backing to the size of the quilt top.

Prepare binding strips the length and width of the quilt plus 2.5 cm (1 in) checking the measurements as you did for the borders. The measurements given in this book include an additional 4 cm (1$\frac{1}{2}$ in) for adjustments. Join pieces, if necessary, to achieve the required length.

Working on the right side of the quilt and with raw edges matching, stitch the binding to the two long sides of the quilt. Turn the folded edge to the back of the quilt. Trim the seam, then attach the remaining strips to the top and bottom of quilt, making sure there is at least 12 mm ($\frac{1}{2}$ in) excess binding at each end. Turn the folded edge of the binding over to the back of the quilt and slipstitch all the binding in place, folding the excess length to cover the raw edges.

Bias strips, cut at an angle of forty-five degrees to the grain of the fabric, can be used to bind your quilt. Join bias strips to achieve the required length.

For bias corners, start the binding near the centre of one of the sides of

the quilt. Leave the first few centimetres loose to overlap later. When you reach the corner, stop the stitching 1 cm ($\frac{3}{8}$ in) from the edge and backstitch. Cut the thread. Fold the binding up and away from the quilt, (Fig. 13) then fold it again so that it is along the next edge of the quilt to be sewn (Fig. 14). Start stitching from the fold in the binding to the next corner and repeat. When you have reached the starting point, overlap the bindings at an angle of forty-five degrees and slipstitch. Turn the binding to the back of the quilt, and slipstitch it in place. At the corners, fold the binding to form mitres on both the front and the back of the quilt and stitch it down.

SIGNING YOUR QUILT

It is essential that you sign and date your work at the very least. But so many lovely old quilts give us no information about them that it would be good to include who the quilt was made for and why, the name of the quilt, where you come from and anything else interesting for future generations. You can type or write on fabric if you iron a piece of plastic-coated freezer paper to it first. Test a sample to be absolutely sure that the ink is permanent. Sew the completed label to the back of the quilt. Alternatively, you can embroider your label, or simply

handwrite it using a permanent marking pen.

CARE OF QUILTS

If you have prewashed your fabrics, your quilt can be washed on a gentle cycle with very mild detergent and tumble-dried on a cool setting. You may hang the quilt in the shade to dry or lay it out flat in a shady place, if you wish. Take the quilt indoors as soon as it is thoroughly dry. Inside the home, keep quilts out of direct sunlight and fluorescent light.

To store your quilt, fold it and place it in a one hundred per cent cotton pillowcase or an acid-free box. Do not store it in plastic. Refold the quilt occasionally so that ridges do not form.

MEASUREMENTS

I have included both imperial and metric measurements throughout this book. For the cutting of quilt pieces which need to be exact, the conversion from one to the other is given as accurately as possible without introducing excessively difficult numbers. The measurements have been adjusted as necessary to ensure that the quilt goes together well.

In cases where the conversion is less critical, such as for fabric quantities, working lengths of fabric borders, the measurements have been rounded out for ease of working. It really does not matter if your border is 3 mm ($\frac{1}{8}$ in) wider than mine!

However, the two sets of figures are not interchangeable. It is important that you work only in one form of measurement for any one quilt–imperial or metric–and don't switch between them.

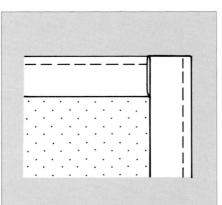

Fig. 13

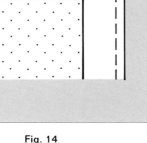

Fig. 14

THE MIRRABOOKA QUILTERS

Back row, from left to right: Carolyn Sullivan, Sue Manchip, Helen Tyler, Evelyn Seymour, Karen Fail
Front Row, from left to right: Dawn Richter, Jenny Searle, Sally Bell, Lea Lane

EDITORIAL
Managing Editor: Judy Poulos
Editorial Assistant: Ella Martin
Editorial Coordinator: Margaret Kelly
Photography: Andrew Payne
Styling: Louise Owens
Illustrations: Lesley Griffith

DESIGN AND PRODUCTION
Managers: Sheridan Carter, Anna Maguire
Design: Jenny Nossal
Photo Editor: Kirsten Holmes
Layout: Sheridan Packer
Cover Design: Jenny Pace

Published by J.B. Fairfax Press Pty Limited
80-82 McLachlan Ave
Rushcutters Bay, Australia 2011
A.C.N. 003 738 430

Formatted by J.B. Fairfax Press Pty Limited

Printed by Toppan Printing Co, Hong Kong
© J.B. Fairfax Press Pty Limited 1995
This book is copyright. No part may be
reproduced by any process without the
written permission of the publisher. Enquiries
should be made in writing to the publisher.

JBFP 412

CREATIVE TRADITIONAL QUILTMAKING
ISBN 1 86343 246 9

FRONT COVER: CHAIR AND BASKETS FROM CANE AND COTTAGE
ANTIQUES, LINDFIELD, NSW; WOOLS AND KNITTING NEEDLES
FROM GRETA'S HANDCRAFT CENTRE, LINDFIELD, NSW.

ACKNOWLEDGMENTS

Many people make a book possible, but this book would
have been impossible without the generosity of the
Mirrabooka Quilters. They not only lent their wonderful quilts
to me during the time it took to write the instructions, but
continually offered their enthusiasm and support. My special
thanks to Jessica who, though only four years old, gave up
her quilt 'Hearts and Flowers' only a week after receiving
it as a birthday gift.

Judy Poulos, my editor, and Sheridan Packer, the layout
artist, shared my enthusiasm for the quilts and made the
project fun, as did Andy Payne, the photographer, who
now claims he would rather go to a quilt show than an art
exhibition. As always, my family Paul, Rachel and Tim,
Emma and Abby offered encouragement and support.